A Critical Jubilee
Selected Essays

Also by the Same Author

Shaw the Novelist 1959
Ernest Hemingway: A Study of his Rhetoric 1983
New Horizons in Teaching English 1992
The Critical Pursuit 1994
Abburi Ramakrishna Rau 2002

Books Edited by the Same Author

Selected Addresses and Papers of the IAAS Conference, Pune, 1987
Mark Twain and Nineteenth Century American Literature 1993
John Keats: An Anthology of Recent Criticism 1993
Ernest Hemingway: Centennial Essays 2000

A Critical Jubilee
Selected Essays

E. Nageswara Rao

AUTHORSPRESS

Worldwide Circulation through Authorspress Global Network
First Published 2004
by Authorspress

E-35/103, Jawahar Park
Laxmi Nagar, Delhi-110 092

e-mail: authorspress@yahoo.com

Typeset in NewCenturySchlbk by Chitra Computers

A Critical Jubilee: Selected Essays
ISBN 81-7273-159-0

Printed in India at Tarun Offset, Delhi.

For

THE ENGLISH PROFESSION

Acknowledgements

The author and the publishers of this volume are grateful to the editors and publishers of the journals and anthologies for permission to reprint articles which originally appeared in them as listed below:

1. "Shaw's Short Stories." *English Studies* 2(1954): 94-101.
2. "The Significance of *Frankenstein*." *Viswabharati Quarterly* 32 (1966-67): 250-258.
3. "Wordsworth and the Cartesian Revolution." *Rajasthan Journal of English Studies* 2(1976): 3-8.
4. "The Other Harmony of Professor Godbole." *Indian Journal of English Studies* 26 (1987): 23-28.
5. "The Fertility Motif in Kamala Markandaya's *Nectar in a Sieve*." *Indian English Literature since Independence*. Ed. K. Ayyappa Paniker. New Delhi: Indian Association for English Studies, 1990. 7-11.
6. "The Making of the American Language." *Indian Contribution to American Studies*. Ed. B.P. Dalal. Bombay: Somaiya, 1992. 7-11.

7. "'Perpetuated Piracy': Mark Twain's Attitude to Monarchy." *Mark Twain and Nineteenth Century American Literature.* Ed. E. Nageswara Rao. Hyderabad: American Studies Research Centre, 1993. 8-16.
8. "An American Passage to South India: The Fiction of Robin White." *Indian Journal of American Studies.* 24.1 (Winter 1994): 23-26.
9. "The Revolutionary as Playwright: Dario Fo's Iconoclastic Art." *Andhra Pradesh Times* (Dec. 28, 1997).
10. "The Hemingway Menagerie." *Journal of the Department of English.* (Rabindra Bharati University, Kolkata) 5 (1999): 74-82.
11. "English Language Teaching in the Twenty-first Century." *IT Revolution, Globalization and the Teaching of English.* Eds. G.Damodar, et al. New Delhi: Atlantic Publishers and Distributors, 2001. 85-89.
12. "John Keats as a Literary Critic." *Literature and Criticism.* 2.1 (April 2002): 21-25.
13. "Canadian Contribution to Literary Criticism." *Modern Literary Criticism: Theory and Practice.* Vol I. Ed. N.D.R.Chandra. Delhi: Authorspress, 2003. 237-243.
14. "Margaret Atwood's Views on Language." *Modern Literary Criticism: Theory and Practice.* Vol I. Ed. N.D.R.Chandra. Delhi: Authorspress, 2003. 243-250.

Preface

This collection of my articles and papers is brought out to commemorate the fiftieth anniversary of my teaching and research career. The present volume contains a selection of my articles written or published in the last five decades in various journals and anthologies. I have selected one piece from each of the first four decades; six articles from my publications in the 90s, and five from the new century. One article, "Huckleberry Finn's Adventures with Women," is awaiting publication. Although the selection is rather arbitrary, it reflects to some extent my literary interests, critical concerns and pedagogical preferences. A dozen of these papers were presented at national/international seminars/conferences. The articles are published here in the chronological order in which they were published since the occasion is the golden jubilee of my career.

I believe a teacher continues to learn throughout his life. He learns through teaching because he has to clarify things for himself before he can communicate his understanding to his students. I also believe that writing is a twin discipline of teaching and that it helps a better understanding of a work or a literary problem. These fifteen essays are a sampling of my attempts at understanding a few of the literary works I savoured in the last half a century. If some of these are found useful to students and teachers of literature elsewhere, it is a matter of great satisfaction to me.

Considering the long span over and different occasions on which these essays were written, there may be variations in rigour and presentation. The original documentation of these articles is retained for convenience, although there are significant changes in the style of documentation over the years. These changes will be evident from the earlier to the later articles in this volume itself.

I wish to express my special thanks and appreciation to my daughter, Swapna, who typed the book with accuracy, neatness and speed.

I am grateful to Authorspress, Delhi, for publishing this book in an attractive format, and in record time.

This book is offered as a small token to repay my debt accumulated over the past fifty years to the English profession.

E.Nageswara Rao

Contents

1

Shaw's Short Stories

Bernard Shaw's literary career mainly consisted of writing imaginative fiction, though the form varied from the novel and the short story to the play. He began writing stories even while he was a small boy in Dublin. One of the earliest of his stories was about a man with a gun who attacked another man in the Glen of the Downs. This and perhaps a few others were published in MS magazines, mostly run by his friends. In 1884, he wrote another story entitled "The Brand of Cain" which is not published even to this day. He explained the story to his secretary some years later from memory. The story was designed to illustrate the notion that things which are not visible to the naked eye come out true in photographs.

Apart from the unpublished stories of which we have no record, we have fourteen items in the Standard Edition entitled *The Black Girl and Some Lesser Tales* (1934). Though they are called 'tales,' some of them are strictly neither tales nor stories. It would be better to describe them as 'scraps and shavings', as Shaw did in his 1932 edition. Pieces like

"Beauty's Duty" and "The Domesticity of Franklyn Barnabas" are both in form and content small plays while "Death of a Revolutionary Hero" and "A Sunday on the Surrey Hills" can at best be described as personal reminiscences. Some of these pieces are obviously intended as 'padding' for this volume. The themes of the stories are also familiar to the students of Shaw's works. The themes of *Man and Superman*, *Back to Methuselah* and *A Doll's House*, blaming the bard, love, religion, atheism, war, music—all these form the subject matter of the stories.

Chronologically, "The Miraculous Revenge" comes first. The graveyard of a Catholic village called Four-Mile Water shifts suddenly by itself from the north side of the Water to the south, consequent to the illegal burial of an atheist. This is the 'miracle' which is sought to be investigated by the Cardinal Archbishop's nephew, Zeno Legge. Zeno finds the miracle true and suggests a committee to enquire into the matter thoroughly. While awaiting the arrival of the committee, he falls in love with the local clergyman's niece, Kate. She discovers that he is the Cardinal's informer. There is a violent row between him and her uncle, Father Hickey. Zeno is physically injured. He vows to take revenge before next morning by undoing the miracle and thus exposing the clergyman to the scorn of the committee. Accordingly, he goes to the cemetery at midnight, exhumes the coffin of the atheist, takes it to the southern side and inters it there. The Catholic cemetery once again goes back to its original habitation on the northern side. Having thus accomplished his revenge, Zeno leaves for Dublin. The clergyman is dismissed as he is found guilty of 'a gross imposture'.

This story is hardly credible. Shaw's aim seems to be to ridicule the self-deceptions of the priestcraft. There is biting sarcasm in the stern refusal of the dead catholic saints to lie in peace with the reprobate. The complacency with which the clergyman bade his fellow men not to interfere with the burial of the atheist on the ground that it is illegal is only Shaw's mockery of the priest's flying in the face of truth. Here it is interesting to note that when Shaw passed away, the interment of his body in the Westminster Abbey and the burial of his ashes in any national shrine had to be given up since it was believed to "wound the feelings of several churchmen"[1]. It is also interesting that Bruce Marshall's novel, *Father Malachy's Miracle* tells much the same story as Shaw's.

The second story, "The Serenade," is about two young men who try to outwit one another in winning the affections of a beautiful lady, Linda Fitznightingale, by singing to her her favourite song, Schubert's serenade. Col. Green, one of the suitors, actually plays it on his horn at midnight before her house. It is not to her taste. Luckily for him, she is under the impression that it was done by the other gentleman. Due to a curious set of circumstances, eventually Linda marries Col. Green. This story is remarkable for its neat plot construction and for the description of the psychology of the rivals. It may be said without hesitation that this is the finest story in this collection.

The third story, "Don Giovanni Explains," is obviously a trial sketch of the Don Juan play, *Man and Superman*. The story of Don Juan's romantic adventures is told by his ghost to a young lady returning home after attending Mozart's opera commemorating him. The ghost insists that he never fell in love with any woman, which fact was sadly overlooked in the play and in the opera. The humorous climax is reached when the lady declares her love even for the ghost of Giovanni. In the play which Shaw wrote six years later, there is a consistent and credible philosophy. He propounded his magnificent doctrine of the Life Force, which became the basis of Creative Evolution. He emphasised his thesis that man is the quarry and woman the huntress in the duel of sex, even in the story. Not only the ideas, but the words also are identical.

The fourth piece, "A Sunday on the Surrey Hills," is only a personal reminiscence of Shaw's visit to his famous vegetarian friend, Henry Salt. It describes his unhappy experiences on a rainy day in the countryside. Despite the great hospitality of his hosts, he felt very irksome. The Salts were like ducks in the rain. It made them happy. This essay is remarkable for the delicate and racy humour of Shaw.

Incidentally, it shows that he has a distinct humour, besides his wit, sarcasm and paradox. It is also an example of his love of detail.

The next item is a sequel to Walter Besant's sequel to Ibsen's *A Doll's House*. Here Shaw describes an interesting conversation between Nora and Krogstad. Nora returns home twenty years after her epoch-making exit. In this interval, her husband became a drunkard, her son a forger and her daughter, Emmy, fell in love with Krogstad's son. When Krogstad told Emmy that he would not allow his son to disgrace himself by marrying a forger's sister, she committed suicide by drowning. Nora exposes the self-deception of all the Directors of the Board and their respectability which is only skin-deep. She also accuses Krogstad of being a male doll in Christine's house. After explaining the difference between his ideal and his wife's ideal and how far they succeeded in realising them, she tells him: "it [marriage] always sacrifices one of the couple to the other or ruins both"[2]. Krogstad replies that it is "men who are the slaves of marriage"[3] in any case. While Besant's sequel is concerned with the vindication of Victorian domestic morality, Shaw's sequel is concerned with the vindication of Nora's morality. He has shown us that there are male doll's houses also. This dialogue is a typical example of the Shavian technique, its outspokenness and explicitness, which is a distinct contrast to Ibsen's technique, its subtlety, suggestiveness, and appalling poignancy.

"Cannonfodder," the sixth story, is actually a collation of three experiences on three different occasions on which the author observed soldiers going to a battlefront. He describes with a penetrating psychology the feelings of the cannonfodder. The Italian conscripts were making merry by singing. The British soldiers were indignant and intensely unhappy at the prospect of war on the first occasion, but later they also behaved much as the Italians. In this story the author wants to drive home that it is difficult to carry on the arts of war or peace by men who do not understand what they are doing. The attitude of the soldiers, whatever may be their nationality, towards war, is one of indifference and unconcern.

The seventh story, "The Theatre of the Future," gives an account of the successful efforts of Gerald Bridges in building a cash-for-admission theatre (as a protest against the West End theatres which required introductions for admissions to the stalls) with the help of some experienced people. The intelligent publicity and the judicious schedule of performances made for the success of this new theatre. This is the third longest story in this anthology and rather monotonous too. The subject matter is hardly suitable for a good story, though humour is used sparingly. Here we come across long-winding sentences, which are a relic of Shaw's early novels. The story is perhaps meant as a dig at the nineteenth and early twentieth century British theatres before he undertook their reform.

The obituary article entitled "Death of an Old Revolutionary Hero" was written as a personal explanation to clear up a misunderstanding. When Joe Budgett, a veteran of the International and a very independent Socialist, died, Shaw was prevented from speaking at the funeral by Mrs. Budgett on the plea that he tried to kill her husband on an earlier occasion. This was the subject matter of some comment in a section of the Labour Press, unaware of the truth of the charge. Shaw gives a detailed account of his interview with the ailing Joe, who was opposed to all the socialist movements of the time for some reason or other. He was a great socialist but he never budged an inch; he never compromised. "All or nothing" was his guiding principle. Sometimes he even went to the extent of joining hands with the reactionaries. Shaw, being a Fabian, could not accept this position. So he annoyed Joe by throwing down a clock and incidentally broke the promise he made to Mrs. Budgett not to make any noise. Shaw had no doubt great respect for Joe's tenacity and singleness of purpose but he could not help mocking at him for his impractical and imprudent steps.

"Aerial Football: The New Game," the next story, is a fantasy which was awarded a thousand-dollar prize by *Collier's Weekly*. Shaw rejected the prize forthwith and wrote a very pungent letter to the editor, taking him to task for assuming that he was in the habit of accepting bonuses and of competing for prizes. The story deals with the experiences of a woman named Mrs. Hairns and the Bishop of St. Pancras in heaven. Mrs. Hairns in spite of her vices on earth is able to secure admission into heaven while the pious clergyman is dissatisfied with it and behaves arrogantly towards the saints including St. Pancras. He keeps the saints and the angels busy with a ball made out of his apron. In this story the arrogance of the clergy is pictured. The temperaments of the Bishop and Mrs. Hairns are vividly described. The denouement focuses our attention on Shaw's open disrespect to religion. Dr. Archibald Henderson[4] tells us that this story is reminiscent of Mark Twain's "Captain Stormfield's Visit to Heaven."

The next story, "A Dressing Room Secret," is part of blaming-the-bard campaign. Shaw takes Shakespeare to task for not clearly thinking out his plays beforehand. Desdemona should have been depicted as a woman of evil reputation, in which case Othello's jealousy would have had a 'natural' reason. Now the misunderstanding is only 'mechanical' and hence the play turned out to be a 'farce'. Lady Macbeth becomes a copy of Ann Hathaway, contrary to the original plan of making her really awful. Poins was meant to be Prince Hal's conscience-keeper, but Falstaff spoiled this. One wonders whether Shaw is at all serious in making these charges. They are frivolous and do not carry conviction.

The eleventh story, "The Emperor and the Little Girl," is suggestive of the deep-seated humanity of a die-hard warmonger. All his sympathy and humanity could be brought out only when he personally witnesses the tragic scene of the battlefield. The Kaiser pleads with a little rescue girl that the destruction is not his doing and that he did not make himself Kaiser. The soldiers, who were responsible for both, deprived him of "natural equality and innocent play of an ordinary human being."[5] The Emperor is only a "Usuality" and is not permitted to do anything unusual. In the portrait of the Emperor is perhaps the root of the Inca of Perusalem.

We have then a long piece brought over from Shaw's favourite play, *Back to Methuselah*. While he was mainly concerned with the extension of human longevity in the play, the domestic history of Franklyn is depicted in this. His domestic life is not happy because his wife Clara could not understand the theory of Creative Evolution, which was propounded by him in collaboration with his brother, Conrad, and a lady friend, Mrs. Etteen. Clara suspects her husband of philandering with Mrs. Etteen and runs away from him and presently comes back. There are first-rate intellectual discussions in this piece. Chesterton is caricatured as Mr. Immenso Champernoon. The whole thing is a delightful and refreshing essay in Creative Evolution.

In the chronological order, "The Adventures of the Black Girl in her Search for God" comes last, but it is the most important story in this collection. That is perhaps the reason for making it the leading story in this book. It was written in South Africa at a place called Knysna, where Mrs. Shaw was convalescing after a motor accident. The indefatigable black girl, 'an interesting and unsatisfactory convert' takes the missionary at her word and goes in search of God. On her way, she meets one after the other, the gods of Noah and Job, Ecclesiastes, Micah, Pavlov, Jesus, the Caravan of the Curious and Mahomet. She is not satisfied with their answers. They fail to explain the incompatibility between the omnipotence of God and the existence of evil in the world. Finally, she meets Voltaire who tells her that God in his divine mercy does not reveal Himself to her, lest too full a knowledge of Him should drive her mad even as Semele was driven to death by the presence of Jupiter. Until we have fulfilled all his purposes, and be gods ourselves, we shall never bear His full presence. We shall not be able to keep pace with His infinite purposes, which failure is really a blessing in disguise for us, since the minute we finish His work, we would be dispensed with as unnecessary. On his advice, the black girl continues her search by restless work in the garden. In course of time, she marries 'a red-haired Irishman' (apparently Shaw). Ever since she is busy with her household duties and bringing up her children. There is hardly time for her divine search now. She even thinks it funny on her part to go in search of God thinking herself to be the centre of the universe.

This story tackles one of the fundamental questions which every thinking person asks himself and offers a Shavian answer that it is puerile and futile to go in search of God, imagining vaingloriously that our individual selves are the centre of this mysterious Universe. We are here to fulfill the mission and purpose of God. Judging from the deep conviction with which this story and its preface were written, one wonders whether Shaw was at all an atheist as he declared on a number of occasions. It is certain that he believed in God, not the popular, conventional, purposeless and irrational notion of God. His conception of God is linked up with Life Force and Creative Evolution[6]. This story may be described as Shaw's religious manifesto and it naturally led him to a dispute with a catholic who asked him to withdraw it from circulation and make a public recantation! Shaw politely replied that a lakh of copies of the story were already sold by then and that the mischief, if any, was already done. He added that he had a "more exalted notion of divinity"[7] than the Catholics.

The above fourteen stories were written over a period of nearly half a century – strictly, forty-seven years – the earliest in 1885 and the latest in 1932. They have neither a common theme nor a common technique. In style there is greater suppleness and facility as we proceed from the earlier to the later stories. The stories are interesting both for their matter and manner; they have a particular value to the students of Shaw. Since Shaw's chief interest was elsewhere, he could not be expected to contribute to the art of story-telling as much as Maupassant, O. Henry, Anton Chekhov and Katherine Mansfield did.

NOTES AND REFERENCES

1. A.C. Ward. *Bernard Shaw*. (Men and Books). London: Longmans. (1951), p.27.
2. George Bernard Shaw. *The Black Girl in Search of God and Some Lesser Tales.* (Standard Edition). London: Constable, (1949). p.208.
3. Ibid. p.211.
4. Archibald Henderson. *Bernard Shaw: Playboy and Prophet*. London: D. Appleton and Company Ltd., (1952). p.114.
5. *The Black Girl.* p.98.
6. The clergyman who offered prayers at Shaw's deathbed declared: "This man was surely no atheist". (See *George Bernard Shaw: A Critical Survey)* (ed.) Louis Kronenberger. New York: The World Publishing Co. (1953). p.257.
7. Blanche Patch. *Thirty Years with G.B.S.* London: Victor Gollancz, (1951). p.195.

2

The Significance of *Frankenstein*

Mary Shelley's *Frankenstein* is an extraordinary novel in many ways. It was the first novel of a nineteen-year-old girl with an unusual background. Mary's mother was the author of the first feminist document, *Vindication of the Rights of Woman*. Her father's *Political Justice* influenced the thought of his time considerably. Her husband was reputed to be an atheist and a socialist. Among her friends was Lord Byron.

Mary wrote *Frankenstein* in Geneva in 1816. Though started as a ghost story, the finished novel is more than that. A multiplicity of themes from a variety of sources[1] are fused in it by linked analogies and repetitive patterns in structure and action. The alternate title, "The Modern Prometheus," focuses our attention on a dominant theme of the novel. Prometheus stole fire from the gods and rebelled against oppression. The poet Shelley was deeply impressed by this spirit of liberty and used this myth in his *Prometheus Unbound* on which he was working at about the same time as his wife was writing her first novel.

Prometheus's modern counterpart, Frankenstein, "stole" another vital secret of the gods by animating a corpse through scientific experiments. He was motivated by a desire for knowledge: "if I could bestow animation on lifeless matter, I might in process of time...renew life where death had apparently devoted the body to corruption."[2]

But he viewed the moment of his triumph as a "catastrophe". He was racked by guilt and fear because of subconscious realisation of his crime against God's creation. His sense of guilt becomes accentuated with every incident in the novel. Because of bitter remorse he abandoned making a female companion for the Monster. He had realised the "wickedness" of his deed, repented for it, and tried to annihilate the monster. In this, the modern Prometheus is rather different from the ancient one.

Frankenstein's guilt introduces the theme of *The Ancient Mariner* into the novel. The hero in Coleridge's poem had killed an Albatross and had brought swift retribution upon himself and his companions. The burden of the lonely mariner's guilty soul could be relieved only by confessing his wicked deed and by communicating his agony to a sympathetic listener. Frankenstein is another version of the travelling mariner. He had not killed any of God's creatures. But he had broken the same divine law indirectly. The Monster was *his* creature and the Monster's crimes were his crimes. His anguish and alienation increase with every murder committed by his creature. When innocent Justine was condemned to death for supposedly killing his brother, Frankenstein says: "Anguish and despair had penetrated into the core of my heart; I bore a hell within me, which nothing could extinguish"(73).

Like Coleridge's mariner, Frankenstein was also tortured by "deep, dark, deathlike solitude". William, Justine, Clerval and Elizabeth were taken away from him by his own creature. He was desolate. His redemption also came through suffering. The death of his relatives and friends, imprisonment, illness, isolation and mental distress have cleansed his soul somewhat. He unburdened his guilt-ridden soul like the ancient mariner by telling his story to Captain Walton.

Frankenstein's alienation from society may be interpreted as a punishment for his attempt to cross human limitations. His intellectual curiosity tempted him to seek forbidden knowledge even as Adam was tempted to eat the fruit of the forbidden tree. Adam lost paradise for his sin. Frankenstein lost his happiness and became a pitiable wanderer. Adam's salvation comes through divine grace; Frankenstein's comes through suffering and confusion.

Mrs.Shelley had used her knowledge of *Paradise Lost* extensively. The forest near Ingolstadt where the old man and his children lived in a cottage is similar to Milton's Garden of Eden and its inhabitants. The cottagers were victims of injustice and ingratitude. Their suffering and exile were caused by the baseness of man to his fellow men. But Adam and Eve were tricked into disobedience to God by Satan.

The portrait of the Monster is a careful blending of Adam and Satan. On reading *Paradise Lost*, the Monster himself observed what he shared with each of them:

> Like Adam, I was apparently united by no link to any other being in existence; but his state was far different from mine in every respect. He had come forth from the hands of God a perfect creature, happy and prosperous, guarded by the especial care of his creator; he was allowed to converse with, and acquire knowledge from beings of a superior nature: but I was wretched, helpless, and alone. Many times I considered Satan as the fitter emblem of my condition; for often, like him, when I viewed the bliss of my protectors [the cottagers], the bitter gall of envy rose within me (112).

Frankenstein refers to his brain-child as the Wretch, Devil, Abhorred Entity, Detested Form, Odious Companion, Horror, Hideous Phantasm and Vile Insect. Most of these terms are descriptions of Milton's Satan. Mary uses some of these expressions in her 1831 preface. Her own attitude to this strange being is indicated by the fact that this creature was never christened and was always called the Monster.

The Monster is clearly meant to be an unusual combination of Adam and Satan. He had epitomised the long, slow development of man's civilised life of many millennia into a few months and had learnt many things very fast. He had developed a thirst for knowledge and was self-educated. Tender feelings of affection welled up in him and he craved for companionship. He had made desperate attempts to befriend the cottagers and others. But his physical appearance terrified and repelled others. Even the cottagers who were themselves victims of injustice denied him friendship. His alienation is even more terrible than his maker's. So he complained bitterly: "Satan had his companions, fellow devils, to admire and encourage him; but I am solitary and abhorred" (112). As for Adam, Eve was there to comfort him. But the Monster was shunned and despised by all mankind including his "father."

He was also a victim of injustice and ingratitude like the cottagers in whose proximity he had lived a very fruitful life. His repulsive shape and consequent isolation were blamed on his creator. His benevolent actions like saving a drowning child were misunderstood and this alienated him even more. He vowed vengeance on his maker and on mankind for his undeserving fate. He persistently questioned his creator as Adam had questioned God:

> Did I request thee, Maker, from my clay
> To mould me Man? Did I solicit thee
> From darkness to promote me...?
>
> *Paradise Lost*, X, 743-745

Frankenstein and the Monster represent a psychological conflict between parent and child. The Monster's revolt and vengeful chase of his maker is a rebellion of creature against creator, a re-enactment of Satan's rebellion against God, a repetition of Adam's disobedience, a reflection of Frankenstein's own violation of the divine law. The Monster had probably greater reason to revolt than any of the others, for as he complained, he did not have any of the advantages that all of them have had. By demanding a female companion, he had asserted his right to happiness.

From chapter V to the end, pursuit is another important theme. In the beginning, the Monster follows Frankenstein wreaking vengeance on him by killing three of his dearest ones. But the murder of Elizabeth, Frankenstein's bride, reverses their roles in the pursuit. It is now Frankenstein who sought out the Monster over ice-bound lands and oceans. While the Monster's vengeful murders and his sudden ghostlike appearances do not look like a consistent pursuit, Frankenstein's difficult journey is presented as a continuous hunt in the last few chapters. Curiously, the hunter was urged and sustained by the hunted.

It is in the course of this two-way chase that we become aware of yet another theme. Frankenstein and the Monster are not really two independent entities. They are "complementary" and "antithetical".[3] The creature is an extension of the creator in that he represents the destructive potentialities latent in Frankenstein. The two may be seen as two aspects of a disintegrated personality, an anticipation of the theme of Dr. Jekyll and Mr. Hyde. Frankenstein becomes a disintegrated personality after his dangerous experiment. He becomes more of an emotional and imaginative person and the Monster represents intellect. In their several confrontations, the Monster's arguments stand out for their unassailable logic.

However, it is wrong to see the Monster as an unfeeling, unthinking robot. He had voiced concern for the poor and the suffering and aired views on political justice and education. He had frequently given expression to his emotions. His affection and jealousy were roused when he observed the life of the cottagers. His compassion made him save a drowning child. He revenges himself on Frankenstein by killing three persons. He had felt hunger and thirst the same way as other humans feel. He even had sexual urges when he saw Felix and Safie making love to one another.

If the Monster is Frankenstein's own reflection, or at least some aspect of him, Captain Walton is a projection of Frankenstein. He too has something in common with Frankenstein. He was bound for "the unexplored regions" in search of dangerous and forbidden knowledge. His quest parallels Frankenstein's earlier quest for the secret of life. Therefore, Frankenstein counsels the Captain:

> Are you mad, my friend?...or whither does your senseless curiosity lead you? Would you also create for yourself and the world a demoniacal enemy? Peace, peace! Learn my miseries, and do not seek to increase your own (189).

Frankenstein and Captain Walton erroneously assume that knowledge is a higher good than love or sympathy and that it can be independent of a compassionate society.[4] Both of them started off with benevolent and selfless motives which tend to degenerate into Satanic pride. Self-glory made Walton nearly endanger the lives of his companions. Observe Frankenstein's admission to Captain Walton:

> When I reflected on the work I had completed, no less a one than the creation of a sensitive and rational animal, I could not rank myself with the herd of common projectors. But this thought, which supported me in the commencement of my career, now serves only to plunge me lower in the dust. All my speculations and hopes are as nothing; and, like the archangel who aspired to omnipotence, I am chained in an eternal hell" (190).

Captain Walton shares with Frankenstein and the Monster, a terrible sense of isolation. He wrote to his sister early in his voyage:

> But I have one want which I have never yet been able to satisfy; and that absence of the object of which I now feel as a most severe evil. I have no friend, Margaret:...I desire the company of a man who could sympathise with me; whose eyes would reply to mine. You may deem me romantic, my dear sister, but I bitterly feel the want of a friend (6-7).

The Monster, Frankenstein and Captain Walton are bound each to the others since they are aspects and segments of the same personality.[5] It is therefore appropriate that they should merge into one another towards the end of the novel.

The narrative structure of the novel is also significantly based on these three principal figures. Captain Walton who was literally on the rim of the world represents the external reality and he starts telling the story of his quest and his encounter with Frankenstein. Then Frankenstein tells his story from chapter I through chapter X. The core of the novel, chapters XI through XVI, is told by the Monster. This narrative pattern may be likened to a series of three concentric circles. The innermost circle represents the Monster and his horrors. The outermost circle represents reality. This Chinese-box structure in the narrative underscores the merging of themes and characters on yet another level.

The foregoing discussion of the themes, characters and structure of *Frankenstein* brings us to the question: Is this a Gothic novel? It has few of the conventions and devices of that genre of fiction. In a Gothic novel, the action takes place in the past, usually in the Middle Ages, in and around a haunted castle. The action in Mrs. Shelley's novel is not in the past, nor is it located in a medieval castle, though some critics tried to establish a tenuous link between it and Frankenstein's laboratory. There is no ghost, though the Monster is ghost-like in his demeanor. There is no monk, no magic and no witchcraft in *Frankenstein*. There is no incest. There are no clanking chains, no trap doors, no underground passages, and no charnel houses in this novel. There are, however, terror and horror, but they are not of the melodramatic variety as in the typical Gothic novel.

But the novel is a powerful tragedy. It is Frankenstein's tragedy presented somewhat in the Greek manner. Frankenstein is exceptional in his intelligence and makes a significant choice, accomplishes something unique with completely good intentions. But once his goal was reached, he swelled with pride on his own admission. It is this *hubris* which, in his judgment, led to his fall.[6] Like the fall of a Greek tragic hero, his destruction was brought through mental anguish. Frankenstein's reanimation of a dead body was a blasphemous act just like Prometheus's act of stealing fire from Zeus or Captain Ahab's vengeful pursuit of a dumb brute. Frankenstein also evokes the emotions of pity and fear, pity for the hero's plight and fear of the monstrosities of his creature.

What then is the true significance of this novel written by a teenager of rare imagination? Its moral implications are important to us in the twentieth century, hundred and fifty years after its first publication. To Mary, the Romantic, the rational mind seemed to be evil, breeding only evil. Hence the Monster who represents the rational mind is presented as abominable.[7] Frankenstein's story is also a reworking of the Faustus myth where a person barters away his soul for doubtful and dangerous knowledge. *Frankenstein* is a tragedy of Mary's own life,[8] of her age, of the irreconcilable conflict between emotion and intellect, faith and doubt, mind and matter, and science and religion. The Space Age has brought this conflict into clear focus once again. Hence *Frankenstein* has a relevant meaning and a significant message to us.

NOTES AND REFERENCES

1. See Burton R. Pollin, "Philosophical and Literary Sources of Frankenstein," *Comparative Literature*, XVII (1965), 98.

2. *Frankenstein; or, The Modern Prometheus* (London, 1831), p. 40. Hereafter citations to this novel will be found in the text.
3. Muriel Spark, *Child of Light* (Hardleigh, 1951), p. 134.
4. M.A. Goldberg, "Moral and Myth in Mrs. Shelley's *Frankenstein*," *Keats-Shelley Journal* VIII, Part I (Winter 1959), p. 33.
5. In Jungian terms, Walton may be identified as the subjective psyche (consciousness), Frankenstein as the personal unconscious, and the Monster as the objective psyche (collective unconscious). These three have a complementary and compensatory relationship.
6. There are few indications of *hubris* in Frankenstein's life after the creation of the Monster, though he reasoned thus.
7. Critics have suggested that Frankenstein is Mary's reproach to her father's and her husband's belief in the 'perfectibility' of man.
8. Mary Graham Lund, "Mary Godwin Shelley and the Monster," *The University of Kansas City Review* XXVII (Summer 1962), p. 253.

3

Wordsworth and the Cartesian Revolution

> there is a dark
> Inscrutable workmanship that reconciles
> Discordant elements, makes them cling together
> In one society.
>
> *The Prelude*[1], I. 341-344

The intellectuals right from the seventeenth century were fascinated by Descartes' philosophy of dualism. The poets of the seventeenth century used the sexual metaphor to reconcile these opposites. In Wordsworth's own day, Coleridge talked of the "reconciliation of opposites" and De Quincey spoke of the "law of antagonism". Wordsworth was also concerned with the polarities he observed in nature and society[2] and he attempted to reconcile these "discordant elements" through his "inscrutable workmanship".

We shall now examine this interaction of the antipodal forces in the themes and imagery of some of the shorter poems of Wordsworth before we consider *The Prelude*. When the poet asks the 'simple' child in "We Are Seven," "Sisters and brothers, little maid/How many may you be?" she insists on including her dead brother and dead sister in her tally. Apparently, she has intimations of the immortality of the souls of her sister Jane and brother John. She refuses to believe in the dichotomy of life and death and unity which the sophisticated and experienced adult makes; she sees the unity and continuity of life rather than its breaking-up[3] . In "Tintern Abbey," the ideas of mutability representing flesh and permanence representing spirit are admirably juxtaposed in the poet and in the scene. The poet has changed a great deal in the five years between his first and second visits to the place. But the scene had remained essentially the same. Wordsworth also contrasts "the coarser pleasures of his boyish days," "aching joys," "dizzy raptures," "glad animal movements" in the lap of nature with "the joy of elevated thoughts." He learns to look on nature as a "spirit"; nature gives him animal pleasure; nature lightens the burden of "this unintelligible world" for the poet and it gives him a sense of inner harmony. The polarities in this poem are clear enough: boy, animal, body, and passion on one side, and adult, poet, spirit and harmony, on the other. Similarly Wordsworth uses images of wild and innocent animals to describe Lucy in "Lucy Gray": "fawn at play," "hare upon the green," "mountain roe." She is associated with the natural growth of things: "The sweetest thing that ever grew" (1.7). Her disappearance is rather mysterious, though adult, rational man might conclude that she has died in the blizzard. But her body is never recovered. She is a "living child"; her "solitary song" is heard whistling through the wind; her mortal coil and immortal spirit are involved in a stormy interplay until they are reunited on her fateful journey. The initial contrast in another poem, "Resolution and Independence," is between immobility and motion. The leech-gatherer is compared to a stone, to a sea-beast basking on a rock or sand. The idea of motion is suggested by such words as "travelled," "roamed," "stirring" the waters of the pool, and "his voice was like a stream." The more subtle contrast is between the outer world of the stone-like leech-gatherer and the inner world of the poet's "troubled" mind. Half-way through the poem we are told that the man is not an immobile bundle of bones, but a messenger of God "to give me human strength, by apt admonishment." He is no longer a heap of inert matter, but he has "so firm a mind" that it shocks the poet into an awakening. In Florence Marsh's words, the poem is a "deliberate movement between subjective and objective worlds, between the world of the self and the world of the flesh."[4]

The dichotomy of matter and mind is expressed in the paradox, "The Child is the Father of the Man," in the intriguing "Immortality Ode." The third stanza in which the birds sing, young lambs bound, cataracts blow and every beast keeps holiday is a reiteration of the sheer animal pleasure in our earthly existence. This is appropriately symbolised by the "Child of Joy". But in the eighth stanza of the ode, the child becomes "Mighty Prophet! Seer Blest!" That is, he moves from a world of the flesh to a world of the spirit. The child represents innocence, the sheer physical joy of living. But the child in Wordsworth's poems generally represents intuitive knowledge of spiritual matters. The grown-up man is in some ways an antithesis of the child. He has experience, he rationalises, and he cannot have the dizzy raptures of childhood. And yet he has developed from the child. Thus a human being reconciles in himself seemingly antagonistic forces and attitudes. This ode speaks, on the one hand, of "dialogues of business, love or strife," and on the other of the "Soul's immensity."

Wordsworth recognised the Cartesian dichotomy because it was an inescapable part of his intellectual and cultural inheritance. But he made a sustained attempt in his short poems and in *The Prelude* to mend the split separating mind and matter. "Tintern Abbey" and "Immortality Ode" are good examples among his short poems of this process of reconciliation of discordant elements. He seems to say that the gratification of the physical appetites of an earlier day are an essential step in the long and inevitable process of realisation of the "sense sublime" of the "Soul's immensity."

In *The Prelude*, Wordsworth narrates how the childhood incident of stealing a bird was followed by "Low breathings coming after me" (I.323). Nature has an ability, he seems to say, to inculcate moral feelings in the child, although the child recognises these feelings only in a primitive way. Similarly, in the episode in which the boy steals a rowboat, nature again becomes a moral force to rectify the child's attitudes (I.380-385). There is an increasing sense in Book I that as consciousness grows in the child the physical universe is exerting a powerful shaping force. All the experiences of his earlier "seed-time" were indeed meaningful. The child's unconscious intercourse with nature has a cumulatively powerful effect on him. It has a great educative power. In the later books of *The Prelude*, where he speaks of the experiences of youth and manhood, there are many signs of a gap between his earthly life and the yearnings of his spirit. His eight-month residence at Cambridge makes him realise the insufficiency of such a life. And he is impelled to read a hidden meaning in everything:

> To every natural form, rock, fruits, or flower,
> Even the loose stones that cover the highway,
> I gave a moral life: I saw them feel,
> Or linked them to some feeling; the great mass
> Lay imbedded in a quickening soul, and all
> That I beheld respired with inward meaning.
>
> (III, 127-132).

The rustic dance in Book IV (ll. 309-319) is a "transient pleasure" and it too is mingled with the poet's "intense desire for meditative peace." There is a sudden moment of preliminary dedication to poetry (ll. 333-337). The meeting with the old soldiers in Book IV reminds him again about worldly cares, of war and its horrors. But the soldier's words, "My trust is in the God of Heaven/And in the eye of him who passes me!" (ll. 459-460), give the poet reassurance. Book VI points up the contrast between the background and training of Wordsworth and of his friend, Coleridge. Although the former had grown up in the country, in rural tranquillity, and the latter had grown up in the city with its din and bustle, yet both of them could collaborate fruitfully in the art of poetry. Again, he feels that the inanimate rocks and streams in the Simplon Pass (VI. 562 ff.) were muttering to the mountaineers. He says that our relation to physical nature comes through the sense which in turn relate it to the mind. But in the highest activity of the mind, sense is extinguished. The imaginative process of retrospection makes us feel a kinship with nature. Thus the flesh and the spirit, the Cartesian antipodes, interact and fuse in the realm of imagination. It is because of a sharp faculty of imagination that he could feel the 'Spirit of Nature' even in "London's vast domain," although he was not particularly attracted by the "blank confusion" of city life:

The soul of Beauty and enduring life
Vouchsafed her inspiration, and diffused,
Through meagre lines and colours, and the press
Of self-destroying, transitory things,
Composure, and ennobling Harmony.

(VII, 767-771)

The Prelude deals with the "growth of a poet's mind" and "growth" is a kind of evolution. The evolution in this instance is one of the poet's conception of the Universal Spirit. In boyhood, he conceives of it rather animistically, a conception which is refined with maturity. He attributes to the Universal Spirit the properties of movement, infinity, life, eternal endurance, power, liberty, and unity. He feels this spirit to be divine:

there recognised
A type, for finite natures. Of the one
Supreme existence, the surpassing life
Which – to the boundaries of time and space,
Of melancholy space and doleful time,
Superior and incapable of change,
Nor touched by welterings of passion – is
And hath the name of, God.

(VI.132-139)

Thus the themes and images of the important short poems and *The Prelude* underscore Wordsworth's deep awareness of the dual principles of flesh and spirit, mutability and permanence, discord and harmony, and this world and the other world. He seeks to unite these sets of, what seemed to him to be, only apparent "contrarieties." Miss Maud Bodkin points out in her *Archetypal Patterns in Poetry*[5] that in the novels of D.H. Lawrence, the interplay of flesh and spirit, of matter and mind, is communicated through the imagery of the plain and the mountain, an interpretation which could be applied with equal relevance to Wordsworth also. In climbing the peak of Mount Snowdon, the climactic incident in *The Prelude,* Wordsworth was not only performing an arduous physical act, but attaining a cherished spiritual ideal.[6] The successful ascent may be interpreted as a happy unification of the claims of the body with those of the spirit. Although Wordsworth reveals his distinct awareness of the Cartesian revolution, by habitually pairing opposites, he denies any real dichotomy between matter and mind because he constantly stresses the existence of "a dark inscrutable workmanship" which unites "discordant elements" in a single society.

NOTES AND REFERENCES

1. All references to Wordsworth's poems are to *William Wordsworth: Selected Poetry*. New York: Modern Library College Edition, 1950.
2. See Charles J Smith, "The Contrarieties: Wordsworth's Dualistic Imagery," *PMLA*, 69 (Dec, 1954), 1181-99; Florence G Marsh, "Resolution and Independence, Stanza XVIII," *Modern Language*

Notes, 70 (Nov., 1955), 488-490; Tony Tanner, "Mountains and Depths – An Approach to Nineteenth Century Dualism," *Review of English Literature*, 3, No.4 (Oct. 1962); Albert S. Gerald, "Dark Passages: Exploring *Tintern Abbey*," *Studies in Romanticism*, 3, No. 1, (Autumn 1963), 10-23.

3. This view is rather close to the Hindu view expressed in the *Bhagavadgita* where the divine preacher likens the body to a garment which is discarded very frequently. The soul is immortal and passes through a long cycle of births and deaths, wearing different physical masks (bodies) depending on one's good or bad deeds in each existence. According to this view, life, at least the life of the spirit, is a continuous process.
4. Op. Cit., p. 490.
5. *Archetypal Patterns in Poetry* (London: Oxford Paperbacks, 1963): p. 293.
6. The climactic incident of *The Prelude* is parallel to the conclusion of *The Mahabharata* where Yudhistir climbs the mythic Mount Meru, the gate of heaven, in his physical body because of his virtuous life. Reaching heaven in the earthly frame is considered the greatest accomplishment for a human being. There is the suggestion of enlightenment to Yudhistir which we see paralleled in Wordsworth when he reached the top of Mount Snowdon.

4

The Other Harmony of Professor Godbole

Critical opinion on Forster's characterization of Professor Godbole is rather sharply divided both in India and abroad. Hindu readers of the novel, with very few exceptions, are unhappy, some even feel outraged, with the portrayal of Godbole. To mention two examples: Nirad C Choudhuri[1] , in an influential essay, thinks that Godbole is a clown. K. Viswanatham[2] considers Godbole a caricature and his characterization unreal and silly. David Schusterman[3] is even more forthright in his denunciation of Godbole and says that the Brahmin "makes for disharmony", and that he is, in fact, "a disruptive force". On the other side of the controversy, Wilfred Stone[4] , C Roland Wagner[5] , T.G. Vaidyanathan[6] , Frederick P. W. McDowell[7] and Brijraj Singh[8] have in their different ways attempted to defend Forster's depiction of Godbole. Neither the denouncers nor the defenders seem to have noted that in Forster's scheme of things Godbole occupies an important place since he (Godbole) is made to represent one of the novelist's most cherished values, namely, Harmony. It appears that Forster throughout his career was engaged in a quest for harmony in life and in art. This paper is an attempt to consider Godbole as representing one type of harmony.

Let us first examine the view that Godbole is a clown. That Forster does not intend Godbole to be a clown or a caricature is at least partly vindicated in the attitude of other important characters in the novel towards him. Dr. Aziz has great respect for him and calls him "the most sincere chap"[9] (9); Fielding likes at least "an occasional scrap of him" (315); Mrs. Moore shows him utmost deference. The narrator in the novel says that Godbole's "whole appearance suggested harmony as if he had reconciled the products of East and West, mental as well as physical, and could never be discomposed" (71). And then, a hundred pages later, "no eye could see what lay at the bottom of the Brahman's mind, and yet he had a mind and heart too, and all his friends trusted him, without knowing why" (173). If Godbole could earn the respect of and inspire confidence among Hindus, Muslims and Christians, surely he is not a figure of fun.

Godbole appears thrice in the novel. (The number three, as Wilfred Stone observes in his insightful study, *The Cave and the Mountain*, is important as it recurs in both theme and structure. For instance, the novel is divided into three parts.

Three important religions, Islam, Hinduism and Christianity, figure in the novel). These three appearances, it may be noted, are evenly distributed in the three parts of the novel. Godbole first appears at Fielding's tea-party; second, soon after the arrest of Dr. Aziz; and third, in the festival of Gokul Ashtami. He also sings thrice. Each of his three appearances has a religious aura about it. Fielding and Mrs. Moore eagerly seek his comments and views. Dr. Aziz, we are told, "always felt like a baby in that strange presence" (300). Godbole's mere physical appearance has had a beneficial influence on people around him.

Let us now consider the impact of the three appearances of Dr. Godbole. When he is asked by Mrs. Moore to describe the caves, he gives negative descriptions: "there are no sculptures at Marabar, they are not holy, and they are not ornamented in any way" (74). It is Dr. Aziz who realises that Godbole is concealing something about the caves. Like the definition of God in Hindu scriptures in terms of *neti*, perhaps the caves could be described only in negative terms for they seem to symbolise the everlasting No, the great Void. If Godbole is enigmatic, so are the caves, so is the echo, so is India to the outsiders.

During this meeting at Fielding's residence, Godbole sings his first song which is described thus: "It was the song of an unknown bird. Only the servants understood it. They began to whisper to one another. The man who was gathering water chestnut came naked out of the tank, his lips parted with delight, disclosing his scarlet tongue" (77-78). The British listeners, Fielding and Mrs. Moore, are inquisitive about the meaning of the song and Godbole explains:

> It was a religious song. I placed myself in the position of a milk-maiden. I say to Shri Krishna: "Come: come to me only." The god refuses to come. I grow humble and say: "Do not come to me only. Multiply yourself into a hundred Krishnas, and let one go to each of my hundred companions, but one, O Lord of the Universe, come to me." He refuses to come (78).

While the impact of this song on Indian, presumably Hindu, servants is immediate and spontaneous, it haunts Mrs. Moore and Miss Quested for at least two weeks. In the section, "Caves", (Chapter 14), the narrator says that this "queer little song" had a soporific effect on the English ladies who had both lived "more or less inside cocoons, where the human spirit slumbers for the most part but. . . not nearly as alert as we pretend" (132). Although the ladies do not understand the song, both of them become "apathetic", that is, they are benumbed. The song produces a narcotic effect on them. There is a linked analogy to this song on "come" in the next section when the narrator says India "calls 'come' through her hundred mouths, through objects ridiculous and august. But come to what? She had never defined. She is not a promise, only an appeal" (135). Godbole's religious song is also an appeal to Shri Krishna to come.

If in Godbole's first appearance, we listen to a "queer little song," in the second, we hear a "queer vague talk with Professor Godbole" (172). This queer talk is actually Godbole's exposition of the problem of evil. He argues:

> Good and evil are different as their names imply. But, in my humble opinion, they are both of them aspects of my Lord. He is present in the one, absent in the other, and the difference between presence and absence is great, as great as my feeble mind can grasp. Yet absence implies presence, absence is non-existence (175).

To a superficial observer, these words may appear as quibbling. When Fielding asks Godbole: "Is Aziz innocent or guilty?" he answers that evil is performed by everyone, including Miss Quested. This may be taken as an evasive or idiosyncratic reply. But the Collector expresses the same view in the very next chapter: "We are to blame (for what happened to Miss Quested) in the sense that we ought to have seen the expedition was insufficiently guaranteed, and stopped it. . . We are all implicated in that sense" (182). Godbole is trying to explain in his own way the teaching of Shri Krishna in the Bhagavad Gita. It is significant that on listening to his "value" talk Fielding was "silent, trying to meditate and rest his brain" (175). He does not dismiss it as a pun as he has done "the symmetrical injunction" (292) of Islam: "'There is no God but God' does not carry us far through the complexities of matter and spirit; it is only a game of words, really, a religious pun, not a religious truth" (269). We should remember that Fielding is credited with a "usual sane view of human intercourse" (242). Clearly, he has mentally conceded that Godbole's "queer vague talk" about good and evil has something to it.

In the festival of Gokul Ashtami where Godbole makes his third and final appearance, he is in his element. He sings his second song, "Tukaram, Tukaram," and later leads a choir singing "Radhakrishna, Radhakrishna," and he completely immerses himself in the festivities. In a mood of ecstasy, Godbole has mystic visions twice of Mrs. Moore and the wasp. He sees all forms of life, all creation as one. Indeed, the festival obliterates the distinctions of caste and rank so that the Sweepers' Band and the privileged sections of Hindu society mingle in the vast crowd: "They loved all men, the whole universe, and scraps of their past, tiny splinters of detail emerged from a moment to melt into the universal warmth" (281). Such ecstasy is possible for Godbole as he is fully involved in the religious atmosphere prevailing in the festival. His is the path of devotion, of total surrender to God. The festival held in honour of Shri Krishna generates Infinite Love which "took upon itself the form of Shri Krishna, and saved the world. All sorrow was annihilated" (283). It is important to note that this festival was witnessed, either in body or in spirit, by almost all the principal characters in the novel. Mrs. Moore not only appears in the mystic vision of Godbole twice, she is also present through her progeny, Stella and Ralph, who are understandably drawn to Hinduism. It is in the festival of Gokul Ashtami celebrating universal love that bridges of understanding could be built, bridges connecting races, religions and nations. The bridge party in Chandrapore accentuated such differences and divided people. Gokul Ashtami, on the other hand, coming as a finale to the course of events in the novel, submerges all distinctions and unites people.

After her terrific experience in the cave Mrs. Moore finds Christianity "talkative" and "that all its divine words from 'Let there be light' to 'It is finished' only amounted to "boum" (148), the echo she had heard in the Marabar Caves. Fielding considers the principal tenet of Islam to be a religious quibble, not a religious truth. The experience in the first cave upsets Mrs. Moore; the echo throws Miss Quested off balance. The whole episode makes the British (except Fielding) nervous; even Fielding is quite worried. On his arrest, Dr. Aziz sobs. During the trial also, people on both sides lose their equanimity and after the trial the English become panicky. But the incidents in the

Marabar caves and the subsequent events in Chandrapore, including the arrest of Dr. Aziz, do not affect Dr. Godbole. He alone does not lose his balance, for, he has the capacity to detach himself from people and events; he alone achieves harmony both within and without.

Harmony, as stated earlier, is one of the principal concerns of Forster. As John Colmer perceptively observes: "The all-embracing theme of harmony appears in a variety of ways, not all of them equally successful. It is explored through the private lives of individuals, through the conflict of classes, through the conflict of national traditions."[10] In an important essay, 'Art for Art's Sake', Forster argues that art by definition must have form or order which is a manifestation of "internal" or "vital" harmony. Art cannot exist without form which creates order. And order, according to Forster, is "something evolved from within, not something imposed from without; it is an internal stability, a vital harmony."[11] Forster distinguishes between two kinds of order or harmony: (i) "the divine order, the mystic harmony, which according to all religions is available for those who can contemplate it. . . . The existence of a divine order, though it cannot be tested, has never been disproved," and (ii) the aesthetic order or harmony which "an artist can create in his own work."[12] The uniqueness of a work of art is because it is "the only material object in the universe which may possess internal harmony.[13]

In *A Passage to India* Forster implicitly juxtaposes the two kinds of harmony. On his visit to Venice, Fielding admires the "harmony between the works of man and the earth that upholds them, the civilisation that has escaped muddle, the spirit in a reasonable form, with flesh and blood subsisting. . . though Venice was not Europe, it was part of the Mediterranean harmony. The Mediterranean is the human norm" (275). Fielding forgot the beauty of form among "idol temples and lumpy hills" in India. Elsewhere in the novel references to the formlessness, disorder, or muddle in India occur almost as a refrain. There is yet another kind of harmony which Forster explicitly mentions early in the novel. During the very first encounter between Godbole and the English visitors, the narrator, as quoted earlier, says, "his whole appearance suggested harmony as if he had reconciled the products of East and West, mental as well as physical, and could never be discomposed" (71). If Venetian art produced beauty of form, as all true art would, Hinduism produced harmony of life in the person of Godbole. John Sayre Martin has rightly observed: "But Venice's beauty is that of art, a Venice without life or movement, a Canaletto view, not the living reality. The spirit of Mau, on the other hand, is the spirit of life: all is life and movement."[14] The harmony of spirit is the more difficult to achieve. Hence this harmony of Godbole is superior.

NOTES AND REFERENCES

1. Nirad C Choudhuri, "Passage to and from India." *Encounter* (London), 2 (June 1954) 19-24.
2. K Viswanatham, "Forster: *A Passage to India*: The Desperate View." in *India in English Fiction*. Waltair: Andhra Univ. Press, 1971, (A.U. Series No.100) pp.90-120.
3. David Schusterman, "The Curious Case of Professor Godbole: *A Passage to India* Re-examined." *PMLA*, 76 (September 1976), 429.
4. Wilfred Stone, *The Cave and the Mountain: A Study of E.M. Forster*. London: Oxford Univ. Press, 1966.
5. C. Roland Wagner, "The Excremental and the Spiritual in *A Passage to India*," *Modern Language Quarterly*, 31 (September 1970), 359-71.
6. T.G. Vaidyanathan, "In Defence of Professor Godbole," in V.A. Shahane, ed. *Focus on Forster's A Passage to India*. New Delhi: Orient Longman, 1975. pp. 45-62.
7. Frederick P.W. McDowell, "Introduction" to his *E.M. Forster: An Annotated Bibliography of Writings About Him*. De Kalb, Ill.: Northern Illinois Univ. Press, 1976.
8. Brijraj Singh, "Mrs. Moore, Professor Godbole and the Supernatural: Some Comments on *A Passage to India*". *Literary Criterion*, 15-2 (1980), 44-53.
9. E.M. Forster, *A Passage to India*. Harmondsworth: Penguin Books, 1961, p.67. All subsequent references are given in the text.
10. John Colmer, *E.M. Forster: The Personal Voice*. London: Routledge and Kegan Paul, 1975, p.94.

11. E.M. Forster, *Two Cheers for Democracy*. New York: Harcourt, Brace and Company, 1951. p.90.
12. Ibid., p.92
13. Ibid.
14. John Sayre Martin, *E.M. Forster: The Endless Journey*. Cambridge: Cambridge Univ. Press, 1976, p.154.

5

The Fertility Motif in Kamala Markandaya's *Nectar in a Sieve*

Criticism of Kamala Markandaya's *Nectar in a Sieve* has so far concerned itself largely with such themes as tradition and change[1], sense of identity[2], and novel of ideas[3]. It seems one of the major motifs of the novel is fertility in various forms and contexts. But this aspect appears to have received hardly any critical attention in discussions of this novel. For instance, S.C. Harrex makes only a passing reference to it when he observes:

> Without idealising the hereditary existence of the peasant, Kamala Markandaya demonstrates that his sense of identity springs from a traditional intimacy with the earth, with nature's cycles of creation, destruction and preservation[4].

The subtitle of the novel, "a novel of rural India," stresses its rural setting and character. The novel deals with the peasants, their activities, problems and anxieties, hopes and expectations, and joys and sorrows. It is therefore natural to find in it an emphasis on rural ethos and rural value system. In this value system, the productivity of the land, the fecundity of men, the fertility of women, or the fruitfulness of the plants is of great importance. The fortunes of the central characters are intimately linked to fertility or sterility of the land and of the people. A variation of this theme is the opposing principles of life and death and of the forces which sustain the one or bring about the other. This paper examines in some detail and depth the treatment of this motif in this novel.

The happiness of Rukmani and her family is dependent on a good harvest and that in turn is dependent on timely and adequate rains. Nathan, Rukmani's husband, is a seasoned farmer and skilled tiller, but he is helpless if the elements are unkind. The year Ira was married, "the monsoon broke early with an evil intensity such as none could remember before." Nathan bemoans, "It is a bad season. The rains have destroyed much of our work."[5] When the rains failed, it was equally disastrous:

> Each day the level of the water dropped and the heads of the paddy hung lower. The river had shrunk to a trickle, the well was dry as a bone. Before long the shoots of the paddy were tipped with brown, even as we watched the stain spread like some terrible disease, choking out the green that meant life to us (72).

A hapless Rukmani, forced to sell away even her clothes to pay the rental to the landlord, explains to

Biswas, the money-lender: "For the earth is parched to dust and all that I grew is dead" (74). Observe the destructive power of the sun:

> The drought continued till we lost count of the time. Day after day the pitiless sun blazed down scorching whatever still struggled to grow and baking the earth hard until at last it split and great irregular fissures gaped in the land. Plants died and the grasses rotted, cattle and sheep crept to the river that was no more and perished there for lack of water, lizards and squirrels lay prone and gasping in the blistering sunlight (77-78).

Nathan is assisted by Rukmani. Their sons occasionally joined in the farming operations to make the soil yield a good harvest. Nathan loves the land; Selvam, his fifth son, does not:

> he had no love for it and in return it did not yield to him. He had a knowledge of crops and seasons, born of experience, but where crops thrived under Nathan's hand, under his they wilted. Despite anxious care, the seed he planted did not sprout, the plants that sprouted did not bear (111).

Rukmani's hand is also lucky, that is, if the elements are merciful and cooperative. She plants pumpkin, sweet potato, brinjal, beans, chillies and so on. Rukmani tends her own small garden, besides helping her husband in the field. She narrates her exhilarating experience:

> And their growth to me was constant wonder – from the time the seed split and first green shoots broke through, to the time when the young buds and fruit began to form. I was young and fanciful then, and it seemed to me that they grew as I did, unconsciously, but each of the dry, hard pellets I held in my palm had within it the very secret of itself, curled tightly within under leaf after protective leaf for safe keeping, fragile, vanishing with the first touch or sight. With each tender seedling that unfurled its small green leaf to my eager gaze, my excitement would rise and mount; winged, wondrous. (12-13)

The need to experience the grain by feeling it is urgent in Ira who had lived on the land since birth: "She went and picked a head of paddy before sitting down beside us. I saw her fingers parting the husk, feeling for the grain within" (93). Seeds and grains which are obvious symbols of fertility have become a means of emotional currency and a means of discipline for Rukmani and Nathan. When Rukmani collapses on realising that she has to live in a mud hut on her arrival at Nathan's village, the husband's way of mitigating her disappointment is to show her a handful of paddy from the granary. After a good harvest, the narrator comments: "The sowing of seed disciplines the body and the sprouting of the seed uplifts the spirit, but there is nothing to equal the rich satisfaction of a gathered harvest" (104). Earlier, when Nathan finds no alternative to selling the seed to pay the landlord, the narrator describes it as "the terrible choice forced upon us; this I knew, yet could not prevent my throat contracting, or force the tears back into their wells" (76). The soil in Nathan's field is rich and he is a hard-working farmer. Yet, the yield, the productivity, is determined by unpredictable factors like timely and adequate rains.

The land is almost an inseparable part of the fecund Nathan. He has sired a beautiful daughter, Irawaddy, and six sons through Rukmani and three more through Kunthi. Rukmani and Nathan pride themselves on their sons. The narrator describes Kunthi's husband as "slow, sturdy, dependable, rather like an ox"(82). This description is given before Rukmani comes to know of the illicit affair between Kunthi and Nathan. The reference to "ox" is perhaps unconscious or intuitive. But its sexual implications cannot be overlooked. Kunthi's husband is impotent like the ox; Rukmani's husband is a virile bull. The outlook of the younger generation is also influenced by the same value system. When Rukmani asks her sons, Arjun and Thambi, who decide to go to Ceylon for more money, why they need more money, one of them replies without hesitation: "Why, to eat our fill, and to marry, and for the sons we shall beget" (64). Fecundity, one may venture to suggest, becomes a measure of wealth even in the eyes of an alien like Kenny. When Nathan is apologetic in welcoming Kenny to his "poor household," Kenny puts him at ease by saying: "yet not so poor, for the women of your house do you credit, and you have begotten five healthy sons" (33).

Like impotence among men, sterility among women is considered unacceptable. A barren woman is like a counterfeit coin which is returned to the owner or discarded as useless. Thus Ira is returned to her parents by her husband: "I have brought her back to you. She is a barren woman... I need sons" (50). Ira does not conceive for more than five years, thus repeating Rukmani's own sterile phase. Because of the shame and social stigma attached to barrenness, the women seek remedies to cure them of it in a clandestine way. Kenny helps out Rukmani and Ira, and both of them conceive later on. Rukmani bears six sons and Ira gives birth to the albino, Sacrabani. Barrenness upsets the married life of Ira who is a beautiful girl; it makes Rukmani seek treatment from Kenny. Her secret visits to him are noticed by Kunthi who threatens to blackmail her during the famine. Rukmani yields to Kunthi's threats. Thus infertility, whether of Rukmani, or of Ira, is responsible for agony and for disruption of a happy family life for the mother and daughter.

In a rural society which sets a high premium on fertility, the people are superstitious. Rukmani's dying mother places in her hand "a small stone lingam, symbol of fertility" and re-assures her, "you will yet bear many sons. I see them, and what the dying see will come to pass. . . be assured, this is no illusion"(18). What a stone symbol could not do, the fertility expert does and thus he becomes a demi-god in the eyes of Rukmani who calls him: "My lord, my benefactor," She bends down to kiss his feet (31). Understandably, Kenny's mind is on fertility agents even on this occasion, for he remarks: "I see you collect dung and take it with you. Is it not for the land?. . . I have seen your women for ever making dung-cakes and burning them and smearing their huts. Yet I thought you would know better, who live by the land yet think of taking from it without giving"(32). It is perhaps not a mere coincidence that the fertility symbol (the stone lingam), the fertility expert (Kenny), and the fertiliser (dung) figure in the same chapter within a space of three pages. It seems the idea of potency or lack of it has so filled the mind of the narrator, Rukmani, that she rues "the mighty impotence of our human endeavour" (42) against the destructive power of the storm.

Apart from the hard work of Nathan in his farm, Rukmani also raises vegetables in the backyard of her house. The joy of the first pumpkin from her own garden made her "pulse beat, the blood, unbidden, came hot and surging to my face" (9). Then she plants beans and other vegetables which grow very well. This fruitfulness of the plants has been a matter of pride, wonder, excitement, pleasure and gratification for Rukmani. But lurking beneath the living plants and ripening fruits is the cobra, terrifying and benumbing her. The pumpkin becomes a symbol of death, of the destruction of life, of terror. Rukmani likens the round and fleshed pumpkins to young women (105). The encounter with the cobra, its deadening impact, etches such a deep scar in her memory that when she returns to her village from the city, the image of the serpent is uppermost in her mind: "The time of in-between (her absence from the village) already a memory, coiled away like a snake within its hole" (189).

Rukmani who bears "healthy" sons also raises "healthy' vegetables. In fact, she uses the image of the "fruit" while proudly referring to her sons: "Four more sons, I borne [sic] in as many years – Thambi, Murugan, Raja and Selvam. It was as if all the pent-up desires of my childless days were now bearing fruit. I was fortunate for they were, without exception, healthy" (22).

The quiet agricultural community is invaded by the tannery with its train of hides, vultures and stench, thus polluting the healthy and pure countryside. The tannery not only disturbs the ecology, but also the economy of the village in a rude way. It brings death, destruction and disruption to Rukmani's family. Her son, Raja, dies in the tannery; it drives away Arjun and Thambi to Ceylon to seek their fortunes there; it is responsible for Ira taking to prostitution.

Nathan and Rukmani abandon the land and the familiar rural community; they migrate to the sterilized and unsympathetic urban society. Ironically, they are both driven to the sterile occupation of breaking stones in the quarry where, unable to cope with the work and the new environment, Nathan dies. When Rukmani returns home, her spirits rise: "I looked about me at the land and it was life to my starving spirit. I felt the earth beneath my feet and wept for happiness" (189).

The novel abounds in terms describing various agricultural operations such as tilling, ploughing, sowing, planting, sprouting and reaping. It is equally rich in the use of words like "paddy," "grain," "seed," "fruit," "shoots" and "flowers". Rukmani recalls with a sense of fulfillment:

> Sowing time was at hand, and I was out all day with Nathan planting the paddy in the drained fields. Corn had to be sown too, the land was ready. My husband ploughed it, steadying the plough behind the two bullocks while I came behind, strewing the seed to either side and sprinkling the earth over the basket at my hip (16).

An equally invigorating moment in Rukmani's life, perhaps the happiest day in her life, was Deepavali when she unites with her husband:

> I stretched myself out beside him, close to him in the darkness, and as we touched he turned abruptly towards me. Words died away, the listening air was still, the black night waited. In

> the straining darkness I felt his body moving with desire, his hands on me were trembling, and I felt my senses opening like a flower to his urgency. I closed my eyes and waited, waited in the darkness while my being filled with a wild ecstatic fluttering, waited for him to come to me (57).

Thus the importance of the productivity of the land, the fecundity of the men, the fertility of the women and the fruitfulness of the plants in rural India is reinforced by the diction, recurring images and linked analogies and presented as mutually supportive of each other in Kamala Markandaya's *Nectar in a Sieve*.

NOTES AND REFERENCES

1. Shiv K Kumar, "Tradition and Change in the Novels of Kamala Markandaya", *Osmania Journal of English Studies*, 7, 2 (1969), pp. 1-9.
2. S.C. Harrex, "A Sense of Identity: The Novels of Kamala Markandaya", *The Journal of Commonwealth Literature*, 6, 1 (1971), pp. 65-78.
3. Barry Argyle, "Kamala Markandaya's *Nectar in a Sieve*", *The Literary Half-Yearly*, 15. 1 (1974), pp. 73-84.
4. Harrex, p. 73.
5. Kamala Markandaya. *Nectar in a Sieve*. Bombay: Jaico, 1973. p.39.

6

The Making of the American Language

Anthropologists and linguists believe that language is the key to a culture. The dividing line between culture and civilization is rather thin and it is hardly possible to define one of these without reference to the other. All the resources of a language – sounds, vocabulary, grammar, syntax and other – reveal the culture of the people who speak that language as their mother tongue. This concept of the inter-relationship of language and culture of the people was summed up by the Sapir-Whorf hypothesis: "language structures reality." If Eskimo has three different words for snow, if some African languages have only two words for the seven colours of the rainbow, if Hopi has no past tense, if English has a large number of transitive verbs, if Indian languages have more kinship terms than English, these features reflect reality as apprehended by the speakers of those languages. The language Americans speak is, by the same token, the key to American culture, American civilization, American experience and American way of life.

With the Declaration of Independence in 1776, there was a strong and persistent demand to sever British and European links in other areas also. There was a great surge of linguistic and cultural patriotism which led to a wide-spread contempt for things British and this included the English speech. The Declaration rejected British authority in government. Patriots like Noah Webster strongly felt the need to separate the American tongue from English: "As an independent nation, our honor requires us to have a system of our own in language as well as government."[1] Statesmen realized that language could be an instrument for forging national solidarity which was urgently needed in the aftermath of Independence. Americans with vision saw that the United States was bound to surpass England in population and wealth, and that its cultural independence would grow from that. Thomas Jefferson observed: "The new circumstances under which we are placed, call for new words, new phrases, and for the transfer of the old words to new objects. An American dialect will therefore be formed."[2] Noah Webster thought that this new dialect would develop into a new language which would be as different from English as Modern Dutch and Danish are from German.[3]

The language of the New World may be traced to the beginnings of colonization in the seventeenth century. The first settlers came to Jamestown, Va., on May 13, 1607; the *Mayflower* brought the Pilgrims to Plymouth, Mass., in Nov. 1620. The language these early settlers spoke and carried with them was the Elizabethan English of Shakespeare, Marlowe, Bacon, Bunyan and Milton. Shakespeare's *Macbeth* was published in 1606 and King James's Bible in 1611. Many of the seventeenth-century features of British English are retained in American speech. For instance, the use of the low, front, unrounded vowel in one hundred fifty words like *ask*, *bath*, *path*, and the retention of the final /r/ in words like *car*, *far*, are relics of Elizabethan pronunciation. Seventeenth century meanings may be found in *fall* (autumn), *mad* (angry), *guess* (think), *to loan* (lend) and *sick* (ill). What is more important is that the colonizers carried with them the Elizabethan linguistic creativity, freedom to coin new words, to experiment with vocabulary and to interchange parts of speech freely. The colonisation of the New World originated with the eventful reign of Queen Elizabeth I, a reign marked by a spirit of freedom and innovation in almost every sphere. Puritan constraints hindered a healthy and natural growth of English in England. The eighteenth-century efforts to "fix" and regulate the English language made by Dr. Samuel Johnson, Jonathan Swift and ill-advised prescriptive grammarians like Robert Lowth also had the same unwholesome effect. Fortunately, English on the other side of the Atlantic escaped such suffocating influences. The same democratic impulse which molded the institutions of the United States has been shaping and enriching the American language which is being replenished and reinvigorated constantly by the speech of the common people.

The American language reflects American culture and values. The speech of the common people permeated American language. H.L. Mencken sources Americanisms to "the argots of the more raffish trades and professions."[4] The new generation born on the American soil was uncouth and iconoclastic; its experience was limited largely to a rough and inhospitable world. Such experience and environment called for enterprise and resourcefulness, not decorum. The landscape, the fauna, the flora and even the inhabitants of the New World, were new. The American Indians numbering more than a million and spread all over the land, spoke 350 languages belonging to twenty-five different families, none of which had any connection with any European tongue known to the immigrants. The impact of these strange languages on American speech is quite visible. American Indian words came in handy for the names of the new fauna and flora such as *chipmunk*, *raccoon*, *sequoia*, and *squash*. The encounters, friendly or otherwise, between the Anglo Saxon race with the French, Spanish and Dutch on the American soil fertilized the American language further.

American speech is also free from the constraints imposed by a rigid hierarchical class system which evolved in England over centuries from an earlier feudal system. The democratic principle of equality which was characteristic of the new nation led to greater uniformity in American language than in British English. Standard English is a class dialect of the educated. It is heard over the BBC and in the Public Schools. This dialect has the disadvantage of losing touch with the masses in the rural areas. George Orwell complained that this variety is "the greatest enemy of English" as it suffers from "social anemia."[5] Writers like Mark Twain recognised the importance of the speech of the masses for sustaining a language and deliberately nourished the colloquial tradition in their writings.

Noah Webster's (1759-1843) contribution in shaping the American language is significant. He gave the "schoolmaster's authority" which the new nation needed to bolster its linguistic morale. He fought the British as a teenager on the battlefield and later in other fields. He lived and worked in a milieu which demanded separate identity for America in all fields including language, literature, education, government and church. As a cultural nationalist, he stressed the importance of being American. He did not think that the American variety of English was in any way inferior to the British. His *Speller* made a great impact on American spelling. It simplified American spelling by getting rid of superfluous letters in words like *color* and *traveler*; it brought spelling more in line with pronunciation in words like *center* and *defense*. The linguistic consequence of Noah Webster's orthographic reforms was that there was greater correspondence between American pronunciation and spelling, the political consequence was that it paved the way for national unity. Webster lectured throughout his country arousing interest in spelling and language. In his *Dissertations on the English Language*, he emphasised how American English was different from British English. He proposed new names like "Federal English," United Statesish," or just "Statesish" for the American language. His greatest achievement, *An American Dictionary of the English Language*, was published in 1828. It was the best work upto the time; it contained 70,000 entries as against 58,000 words in Dr. Johnson's dictionary. Webster's dictionary made such a great impact on American culture that the name, Webster, became synonymous with a dictionary in the United States. It produced uniformity and standardisation which were considered desirable goals for the American language. Although Webster faced opposition from bigots and pedagogues and was described as "a pusillanimous, half-begotten, self-dubbed patriot,"[6] his *Dictionary* truly reflected the milieu in which it was compiled. It achieved its two-fold aim of celebrating American life and of enlarging its independence.

After Webster, H.L. Mencken (1880-1965) championed the cause of the American language. Although he too, like Webster, was not a trained linguist, his deep interest in language made him produce a monumental and systematic study, *The American Language*, in 1919. It dealt with all aspects of language and went through four editions and two supplements. In the fourth edition which appeared in 1936, Mencken asked, "Why [should] a dialect spoken almost uniformly by nearly 125,000,000 people yield anything to the dialect of a small minority in a nation of 45,000,000?" He prophesied that future scholars might well study "English" as a dialect of "American."[7]

Although it is difficult to assign the status of an independent language to American speech, there are unmistakable signs that it has an edge over British English. In 1600, English was spoken only in England, and that too as a first language by an estimated seven million people. Now there are 350 million native speakers of English in many other countries. More importantly, nearly 1500 million people use English all over the world. Thus the native speakers are outnumbered four times. This rapid growth in the number of users of English as a second language occurred in the last three decades.

The role of the United States in the vast and rapid spread of English is great. America's political and economic power, prestige, patronage and influence, particularly after World War II, are important factors. The global leadership that the U.S. has assumed in many vital sectors makes it imperative that its language also enjoys a global currency and prestige.

NOTES AND REFERENCES

1. Noah Webster. *Dissertations on the English Language*. Boston: I. Thomas and Co. 1789. 20.
2. Quoted in H.L. Mencken. *The American Language*. Third Edition. New York: Alfred K Knopf, 1930.
3. Webster. 22-23.
4. H.L. Mencken: "The American Language" in Robert E. Spiller, et al (Editors). *Literary History of the United States*. Fourth edition. Revised. New York: Macmillan, 1974. 669.
5. Quoted in George H. Douglas. *H.L. Mencken*. Hamden: Archon, 1978. 59-60.
6. Charlton Laird. *Language in America*. Englewood-Cliffs, N.J.: Prentice-Hall, 1970. 279.
7. H.L. Mencken. *The American Language*. Fourth Edition. New York: Alfred K Knopf, 1990. 609.

7

"Perpetuated Piracy": Mark Twain's Attitude to Monarchy

In at least three of his novels, *The Prince and the Pauper* (1882), *Adventures of Huckleberry Finn* (1885) and *A Connecticut Yankee in King Arthur's Court* (1889), Mark Twain was seriously concerned with the institution of monarchy. In his non-fiction works such as *Roughing It* (1872), *Handbook* (1957), *Autobiography* (1959) and in some of his letters, there are candid descriptions and criticisms of royalty. James M. Cox (1960) traces the anti-monarchical views back to the beginnings of Twain's career in 1866 when Twain attacked feudalism in Sandwich Islands.

In spite of the strong views expressed in different ways such as parody, caricature and satire on monarchy in so many of his works, there is surprisingly very little critical attention paid to this aspect of Twain's work. James Cox (1960) in an article in the *Yale Review* notes Twain's strong prejudice against monarchy; John DeWilt McKee (1960) in a brief essay makes only a cursory reference to Twain's criticism of royalty; Hamlin Hill in his "Introduction" (1963) to *A Connecticut Yankee in King Arthur's Court* comments on Twain's treatment of regal ways; Isaac Sequeira (1991) in a recent article discusses monarchy as one of the triad of medieval British institutions which attracted Twain's disapproval. This paper proposes to consider the attitude of Mark Twain to monarchy in some depth and detail from the evidence available in his fiction and non-fiction. The characters, incidents and dialogues in fiction may be taken by most readers as essential ingredients in the art of make-believe that fiction is. But the testimony provided by a number of non-fiction works spread over Twain's whole career makes one suspect that there is something more to it than the mere demands of fictional art.

Twain was amused by the ways of the royal family of Hawaii. He describes them in *Roughing It*:

> In our country, children play 'keep house'; and in the same high-sounding, but miniature way the grown folk here [Hawaii] with the poor little material of slender territory and meagre population, play 'empire'. There is his royal Majesty the King, with a New York detective's income of thirty or thirty-five thousand dollars a year from the 'royal civil list' and the 'royal domain'. He lives in a two-story frame 'palace'.

And there is the 'royal family' – the customary hive of royal brothers, sisters, cousins and other noble drones and vagrants usual to monarchy, all with a spoon in the national pap-dish, and all bearing such titles as his or her Royal Highness the Prince or Princess so-and-so (486). A small tract of ten acres is glorified as a "kingdom" by the Hawaiians. The gaudy costumes worn by the royalty were even more ludicrous. Twain comments:

> There is a strictly defined 'court costume' of so 'stunning' a nature that it would make the clown in a circus look tame and commonplace by comparison; and each Hawaiian official dignitary has a gorgeous vari-colored, gold-laced uniform peculiar to his office – no two of them are alike, and it is hard to tell which one is the 'loudest'. The King has a 'drawing room' at stated intervals, like other monarchs, and when these varied uniforms congregate there, weak-eyed people have to contemplate the spectacle through smoked glass (489).

Twain points out the pretentiousness, pomposity, pelf, the grossness and gaudiness of the royal households.

In his first fictional attempt concerned with the kings, *The Prince and the Pauper*, he tries to prove that clothes, the trappings of office, rather than the accident of birth, make all the difference between a prince and a pauper. There was striking resemblance between Prince Edward VI, the nine-year-old son of Henry VIII and Jane Seymour, and Tom Canty, a beggar-boy. Their hair, eyes, voices, manner, form, stature, face and countenance matched so well that the Prince remarks to his double: "Fared we forth naked, there is none could say which was you, and which the Prince of Wales" (18). In fact, as the narrator comments, both of them were "so marvellously twinned" (47). When they exchange their clothes, their fortunes also changed correspondingly. Edward was

> no longer a petted prince in a palace, with the adoring eyes of a nation upon him, but a pauper, an outcast, clothed in rags, prisoner in a den fit only for beasts, and consorting with thieves and beggars (70).

Nobody believes his assertions that he is of royal blood and heir to the throne of England. "His clothes were against him" and he becomes a "regal, ragged vagrant" (190-191). Tom Canty, the pauper in royal robes, adapts himself to the new life-style in the king's palace: "He lost his fears, his misgivings faded out and died; his embarrassments departed, and gave place to an easy and confident bearing" (255). While the true Prince learns the hard way that "the world is made wrong, kings should go to school to their own laws, at times, and learn mercy" (244), Tom follows the law of mercy rather than of blood. He saves the Duke of Norfolk from the gallows; he makes war on the unjust laws of the realm; he commands his royal sister, Lady Mary, "to beseech God to take away the stone that was in her breast, and give her a human heart" (257). Because of his initial confusion, hesitation and qualms in the royal palace, he is mistaken to be out of mind. But this condition did not deter the King from declaring with a finality: "Mad or sane still shall he reign" (33). Sanity, then, is not an essential requirement for the office of Kingship and Henry VIII was himself known for his eccentricities.

It is, however, in *Adventures of Huckleberry Finn* that Twain makes a scathing attack on the institution of monarchy. In this novel, there are two separate discussions between Huck and Jim on royalty. The characterisation of the king and the duke throughout the novel is further proof of the author's attitude to the royal pedigree, pretensions, and behavior. As part of the "truck" from *Walter Scott*, Huck gets some books about "Kings, and dukes and earls and such" which he reads to his ignorant and naïve companion, Jim. Twain's initial complaints against royalty and nobility, voiced in this novel through Huck Finn, seem to be: 'how gaudy they dressed, and how much style they put on, and called each other your majesty, and your grace, and your lordship, and so on, `stead of mister" (64). Twain is critical of the way in which the kings do nothing most of the time and yet everything belongs to them. Jim asks Huck:

> En what they got to do, Huck?
>
> They don't do nothing! Why, how you talk. They just set around. . . Except maybe when there's a war; then they go to the war. But other times they just lazy around; ... they fuss with the parlyament; . . . and mostly hang around the harem (64).

The dispossessed kings, Huck explains to Jim, "gets on the police, and some of them learns people how to talk French" (66). The immediate reference in Huck's speech is to the Dauphin who is believed to have escaped from a French prison and gone to America. Some of them are actually involved in illegal and criminal activities. The dividing line between kings and highway robbers is rather thin. Indeed, as Huck remarks, "you couldn't tell them from the real kind."

In the second discussion on royalty, in the context of the Royal Nonesuch performance of the king and the duke, Jim expresses surprise and says: "dese kings o' ourn is regular rapscallions." Huck answers that he is not surprised "because it's in the breed. I reckon they're all alike. . . all kings is mostly rapscallions, as fur as I can make out" (123). Jim in his innocence believes the king and the duke are real and judges that royalty would behave the same way as do the two pretenders on the raft. Twain's satiric barb is in Huck's seemingly naïve assertion that their irksome companions, the "low-down humbugs," are "one of the cleanest I've struck in history." To support his contention, he says that King Henry VIII would have

> fooled that town [Bricksville] a heap worse than ourn done. I don't say that ourn is lambs, because they ain't, when you come right down to the cold facts, but they ain't nothing to *that* old ram, anyway. All I say is, kings is kings, and you got to make allowances. Take them all around, they're a mighty ornery lot. It's the way they're raised (123-124).

Although Huck knows that the intruders on the raft are not real kings, he does not attempt to convince Jim as the latter cannot understand it. Moreover, Huck feels that there is hardly any difference between the real and the fake varieties of royalty. What Huck had read about kings in books had been enacted vividly on the raft very soon. Twain stresses how Huck's bookish knowledge is corroborated by his own experience. In spite of all the deceptions of the king and the duke, Huck is prepared to make allowances for their reprehensible behavior by finding excuses in their breeding. He even wants to return good for evil by trying to save them in the end. But Jim, who was not an eyewitness to most of the felonies of the pair on the shore, detests them more. He couldn't make any allowances, "I don't hanker for no mo`un um Huck. Dese is all I can stan" (124). Earlier, he dismissed even King Solomon as a foolish king on two counts. As he says, "would a wise man want to live in de mids er sich a blim-blammin' [a harem of a million wives who quarrel 'considerable'] all de time? No – 'deed he wouldn't!" Jim also thinks that Solomon's famous judgement on chopping a child into two was anything but wise because as Jim says, "en dey ain't no sense in sich doin's as dat. De' spute warn't 'bout a half a chile, de'spute was 'bout a whole chile" (65).

This outspoken criticism of royalty is underscored by Twain's characterisation of the king and the duke. True to their kind, they compete with one another in tracing their descent back to kings and dukes. They not only establish an order of precedence between them, but disturb the democratic principle of equality on the raft by a single fraudulent stroke of impersonation. In the process they usurp – maybe in the right royal fashion – the (straw tick and corn shuck tick) beds of Huck and Jim in the wigwam. Twain depicts the king and the duke as roving frauds who successfully hoodwink hundreds of gullible people in the towns down the Mississippi. The king "works" the Pokeville camp-meeting, pretending to be a pirate who is instantly and thoroughly reformed by the preacher.

Twain exposes the pretensions, eccentricities, deceptions, cruelties, and vices of the royalty by letting adolescent and naïve characters like Huck and Jim express their revulsion at their behaviour. This exposure is further emphasised by naming the two confidence men appropriately, the king and the duke, characters whose behaviour, one may venture to suggest, is a parody of the behaviour of real kings and noblemen. It is, perhaps, not without significance that the successful defrauding of a whole town, Bricksville, is called the Royal Nonesuch. Twain defines monarchy as "perpetuated piracy" (*Notebook*, 197), and the king describes himself as a pirate straight from the Indian Ocean.

While Twain seems to be concerned with illustrating how the apparel oft doth proclaim the King in *The Prince and the Pauper*, in *Adventures of Huckleberry Finn*, he depicts royalty as confidence tricksters who dupe large numbers of people and live off the people. He mounts a full-scale attack on monarchy in *A Connecticut Yankee in King Arthur's Court*. Although the novel is in the form of a fantasy in that a nineteenth century Yankee travels back in time to the sixth century England of King Arthur, every facet of kingship comes under severe attack. For centuries, kings have harped on their divine appointment so that their throne could be supported by the superstitious people. But when a king's touch fails to cure scrofula (or king's evil), it becomes obvious that divinity does not hedge a king. The Yankee observes:

> There is nothing diviner about a king than there is about a tramp, after all. He is just a cheap and hollow artificiality when you don't know he is a

> king. But reveal his quality, and dear me it takes your very breath away to look at him. I reckon we are all fools. Born so, no doubt (451).

The ignorance and gullibility of their subjects keep the kings on their thrones. There is nothing great or noble in the origin of royal dynasties. Twain explains:

> Chiefs rise by the one divine right – capacity, merit. One of these shows merit for war and government above all the rest, he conspires with a faction of the chiefs and is made king. . . The conspirators make the succession permanent in this king's family, and the crime is complete (*Notebook*, 197).

Most members of the royalty are good for nothing. The "seventh-rate people" figuring as British aristocracies are "a company of monarchs and nobles who, as a rule, would have achieved only poverty and obscurity if left, like their betters, to their own exertions" (*A Connecticut Yankee*, 98). Monarchy demands loyalty to institutions from its people, but not to the country. "To be loyal to rags, to shout for rags, to worship rags, to die for rags – that is a loyalty of unreason, it is pure animal; it belongs to monarchy, was invented by monarchy" (159). The size of kingdoms is ridiculed by Twain: "'Kings' and 'Kingdoms' were as thick in Britain as they had been in little Palestine in Joshua's time, when people had to sleep with their knees pulled up because they couldn't stretch out without a passport" (193). Even a tiny principality is enough for a king to enjoy rights and privileges at the expense of the people.

Royalty are trained to behave in a particular fashion. It is not nature or heredity that they are cruel or without compassion. Morgan Le Fay, accoridng to the Yankee, was more "an ass" by her training. She feels that it is "no crime" but her "right" to kill the page. "She was the result of generations of training in the unexamined and unassailed belief that the law which permitted her to kill a subject when she chose was a perfectly right and righteous one" (217). "She [the queen] was a Vesuvius. As a favor, she might consent to warm a flock of sparrow for you, but then she might take that very opportunity to turn herself loose and bury a city" (220). The brutality and cruelty of the kings and queens is very severe. One man is sent to jail for a mere remark:

> He said he believed that men were about all alike, and one man as good as another, barring clothes. He said he believed that if you were to strip the nation naked and send a stranger through the crowd, he couldn't tell the king from a quack doctor, nor a duke from a hotel clerk (223).

Twain feels that a democracy where every man has a vote is an insurance against brutal laws. "Even the best governed and most free and most enlightened monarchy is still behind the best condition attainable by its people" (320).

The style a king puts on is another butt of Twain's criticism. The slave-owner tries to take the style out of King Arthur to make him marketable. The Yankee remarks: "I had found it a sufficiently difficult job to reduce the king's style to a peasant's style, even when he was a willing and anxious pupil; now then. To undertake to reduce the king's style to a slave's style – and by force – go to! It was a stately contract" (457). The slave driver finds that whatever damage the lash and club and fist do to the king's body, they could not impair his style.

Twain pokes such fun at kings that he presents an amusing argument between the Yankee and Clarence:

> I urged that kings were dangerous. He said, they have cats. He was sure that a royal family of cats would answer every purpose. They would be as useful as any other royal family, they would know as much, they would have the same virtues and the same treacheries, the same disposition to get up shindies with other royal cats, they would be laughable vain and absurd and never know it, they would be wholly inexpensive; finally, they would have as sound a divine right as any other royal house, and Tom VII, or Tom XI, or Tom XIV by the grace of God King, "would sound as well as it would when applied

> to the ordinary royal tomcat with tights on." "And as a rule," said he [Clarence], in his neat modern English, "the character of these cats would be an immense moral advantage to the nation, for the reason that a nation always models its morals after its monarch's. The worship of royalty being found in unreason, these graceful and harmless cats would easily become as sacred as any other royalties, and indeed more so, because it would presently be noticed that they hanged nobody, beheaded nobody, imprisoned nobody, inflicted no cruelties or injustices of any sort, and so must be worthy of a deeper love and reverence than the customary human king, and would certainly get it (514-515).

Twain's depiction of kings and their ways is not simply a matter of story-telling to entertain the public. He expresses the same views on monarchy with greater force in his non-fiction works. He states in his *Notebook*:

> The kingly office is entitled to no respect. It was originally procured by the highwayman's methods; it remains a perpetuated crime. It is no more entitled to respect than the flag of a pirate. A monarch when good is entitled to the consideration which we accord to a pirate who keeps Sunday School between crimes; when bad he is entitled to none at all. But if you cross a king with a prostitute the resulting mongrel perfectly satisfies the English idea of nobility. The ducal houses of Great Britain of today are mainly derived from this gaudy combination (196).

Twain is very clear on the nexus between kingship and crime. He has repeatedly likened kingship to highway robbery and piracy. He is forthright about the criminal origins of a throne: "There was never a throne which did not represent a crime; there is no throne today which does not represent a crime. A monarchy is perpetuated piracy. In its escutcheon should always be the skull and crossbones" (197). He considers kingship as the "transparentest" (196) of all sham and frauds. In reacting to the fall of the Brazilian monarchy, he writes to Sylvester Baxter of the *Boston Herald*: "I believe I should really see the end of what is surely the grotesquest of all the swindles ever invented by man – monarchy" (*Letters*).

To summarise: Twain criticises monarchy on grounds of pretended divinity, gaudy dress, presumptuous titles, arrogant style, wrong training or breeding, idleness, greed, meanness, cruelty and lack of compassion and understanding. His main objection to this institution is that it depends on "the misery of the many for the happiness of the few, the cold and hunger and overworking of the useful [so] that the useless may live in luxury and idleness" (quoted in *Handbook* 372). He also objected to kingship because it is unrepresentative of the will of the people; it does not have the consent of the governed. In a hereditary system, the subjects have to endure untold miseries, injustices, brutalities and the whims and fancies of the ruler. A democracy is a better form of government because it represents the will of those governed and the rulers can be changed periodically. The chances of brutal and inhuman behaviour on the part of the rulers are fewer in an elective system.

Twain's attitude seems to have been shaped by American history and American experience. He is influenced by the ideals enshrined in the Declaration of Independence. He is also deeply moved by the French Revolution. He read Carlyle's *French Revolution* avidly. He praised Napoleon for doing away with monarchy and tyranny:

> Bonaparte instituted the setting of merit above birth, and also so completely stripped divinity from royalty that, whereas crowned heads in Europe were gods before, they are only men since, and can never be gods again, but only figure-heads, and answerable for their acts like common clay. Such benefactions as these compensate the temporary harm which Bonaparte and the Revolution did, and leave the world in debt to them for these great and permanent services to liberty, humanity and progress (*Life on the Mississippi*, 374-375).

While Twain was uncompromising on the issue of monarchy, he did respect individual monarchs such as Empress Elizabeth of Austria who was murdered in 1898 and Queen Victoria. It is the system, not so much the individuals, that he despised. Towards the end of his career, when he became increasingly pessimistic about man and his innate nature, he suspected that democracy may gradually revert to monarchy:

> Human nature being what it is, I suppose we must expect to drift into monarchy by and by. It is a saddening thought but we cannot change our nature – we are all alike, we human beings; and in our blood and bone, and ineradicably, we carry the seeds out of which monarchies and aristocracies are grown: worship of gauds, titles, distinctions, power… In public we scoff at titles and hereditary privilege but privately we hanker after them (quoted in *Twain At Your Fingertips*, 282-283).

And if that happens, mankind will have forgotten the lessons of history and forgiven the frauds, shams, scoundrelisms, grotesqueries, brutalities, injustices and cruelties of monarchy.

WORKS CITED

Cox, James M. "*A Connecticut Yankee in King Arthur's Court*: The Machinery of Self-Preservation." *Yale Review* (Autumn 1960), 89-102.

Hill, Hamlin. "Introduction" to *A Connecticut Yankee in King Arthur's Court*. San Francisco: Chandler, 1963.

Mark Twain At Your Fingertips (ed.) Caroline Thomas Harnsberger. New York: Beechhurst, 1948.

McKee, John DeWilt. "*A Connecticut Yankee* as a Revolutionary Document." *Mark Twain Journal*, XI (1960), 18-20, 24.

Sequeira, Isaac. "Mark Twain's Attack on Monarchy, the Aristocracy and the Church in Arthurian England" in *Popular Culture: East and West*. Delhi, B.R. Publishing Company, 1991. pp.71-82.

Twain, Mark. *A Connecticut Yankee in King Arthur's Court*. San Francisco: Chandler, 1963.

__________. *Adventures of Huckleberry Finn*. (ed.) Sculley Bradley, et al. New York: Norton, 1962.

__________. *The Autobiography* (ed.) Charles Neider. New York: Harper, 1959.

__________. *Handbook* (ed.) E. Hudson Long. New York: Hendricks House, 1957.

__________. *Life on the Mississippi*. New York: Harper, .1951.

__________. *Notebook*. Prepared for publication with comments by A.B. Paine. New York/London: Harper, 1935.

__________ *The Prince and the Pauper: A Tale for Young People of All Ages*. New York/London: Harper, 1903.

__________. *Roughing It*. Hartford, Conn.: The American Publishing Company, 1900.

__________. *The Selected Letters* (ed.) Charles Neider. New York: Harper, 1982.

8

An American Passage to South India: The Fiction of Robin White

Robin White is different from many Western writers on India in several ways. He is not an Englishman harbouring a master-slave relationship with Indians; he is not an apologist for imperialism; he does not write on North India. He is not, as he puts it, one of the "I traveled-to-India writers who have capitalized on the Indian scene (mostly to its detriment) and on Western ignorance of it" (White 1963:59). He claims, with some justification, that he is one of the few Western novelists to write on India with a fresh perspective.

Among the Western writers on India, Rudyard Kipling was perhaps the most prominent. Born in India and educated in England, he returned to India at the age of eighteen, and wrote a number of stories and novels on India. As a supporter of British imperialism, his work deals with the theme of the Empire in its finest hour; his fiction presents the life of the British and a few glimpses of the natives and their strange ways. Apparently, he did not foresee any possibility of the British and Indians understanding each other. His statement "East is East and West is West and never the twain shall meet" has become a cliché now. Kipling's perception of the East-West encounter, or rather, the absence of a meaningful interaction, is perhaps typical of an Englishman's view a hundred years ago, given the social, political and cultural environment prevaling then both in India and in England. White (ibidem:58) says: "Kipling possessed a rather parochial view of northern India at the turn of the century, the heyday of the 'Empah'."

Unlike Kipling, E.M. Forster, another well-known British writer, was neither born in India nor did he live in India for long years. He wrote *A Passage to India* after a short visit to India. He chose to deal with the East-West or more specifically, the Indo-British engagement. Although Forster's novel was published twenty-three years before the end of British rule in India, he did not hold out much hope for friendly and fruitful interaction between the British and the Indians. Fielding's efforts in *A Passage to India* to build bridges of understanding between antagonistic ethnic and cultural groups have come to nought. The liberal-minded Forster who had, perhaps, a better insight than Kipling into the nature of Indo-British relations, did not go as far as the die-hard imperialist in predicting the impossibility of the East and West ever coming together. Forster seems to have devoutly wished such a salutary consummation, but he felt that it would not take place soon. His reading of the situation during the twilight of the empire was: "No, not yet."

Both Kipling and Forster, the better known of the Western novelists with Indian theme and locale, limited their canvas to North India where the British were very much in command, with the inevitable consequence of a deeply ingrained feeling of the master-slave relationship among many of the characters they created. Robin White was born and raised in South India; as an American he did not have the same attitude towards India as the British might have had. Unlike Kipling and Forster, he wrote about free India and its people; unlike many others, he chose to write on South India. He firmly believed that:

> there is an enormous difference between being born and brought up in and of a country and just traveling to it on a student or tourist visa. Twain was a tourist; I grew from the soil. On the other hand I would be a tourist on the Mississippi, while that river was the artery of Twain's existence (Letter from Robin White to E Nageswara Rao, 28 August 1964).

Breaking new ground by writing on free India, by locating his stories in Tamil Nadu, by examining the Indo-American encounter, White wrote three novels – *House of Many Rooms* (1956), *Elephant Hill* (1959), and *Men and Angels* (1962). Some of his stories with Indian themes were issued in a volume entitled *Foreign Soil* (1962). In these works, it was White's

> painful privilege to chronicle the decay and demise of Victorian colonialism as seen from the perspective of the missions to India—and I doubt that anyone has ever touched upon a more important shift in world history in terms of interpersonal relations (ibidem).

In the novels and stories, American missionaries play an important role. *House of Many Rooms* is a series of sketches of an American mission family, the Fishers, in an Indian village, that uncover points of interaction between two cultures, two faiths, two ways of life. The result of the Fishers' multifarious involvements with India's custom and belief patterns is sometimes amusing, sometimes sad. Rev. Mr. Fisher confronts a dancing girl who lies across his door as he prepares his sermons. Barney, aged six, speaks with a Hindu ghost. Aaron, seventeen, is keen on becoming a "holy man" and squats for months at the town gates. Mrs. Fisher negotiates the marriage of her Indian butler. The house of many rooms is the Fishers' house in Meigudy to which Mrs. Fisher returns as a lone pilgrim after all her children leave her. The house which throbbed with life is now a house of many vacant rooms. The author explains in a letter to the present writer:

> The spiritual and cultural life of the family of the Fishers was ...consumed by the Hindu milieu, just as Victorian colonialism dissolved under contact with the stronger [Indian] culture (ibidem).

In his next novel, *Elephant Hill*, the central question concerns the conflicting claims to the child, Muthu. The name means pearl and it is in a thematic sense equated with India herself. White (ibidem) sees the sense of contest over the custody of Muthu as the next logical step in his "chronicle of the decay and demise of Victorian colonialism." In the novel, East meets West with all the possible suspicions and misunderstandings, finally leading to mutual respect and love. Muthu is the illegitimate son of Alagarsami; he is adopted by an American mission family, the Westmores. Alagarsami is keen on the claims because he is a widower without a legal heir. His uncle threatens to transfer his business to a distant cousin if Alagarsami does not have a son; his mother opposes a second marriage. Bullied by a despotic uncle and a domineering mother, he makes his claim on Muthu in a tactless manner. Though the Westmores had their own children subsequent to their adoption of Muthu, they have become so attached to the Indian boy over the years that they find it hard to give him up. This dispute assumes ridiculously huge proportions. Alagarsami resorts to legal action and even denies the right of way to the Westmores to their residence. Every word, deed and gesture on either side is misunderstood and suspected by the other side. The atmosphere of distrust is intensified by several cleverly contrived situations. Miss Summer, Mrs. Westmore's sister, who tries to reconcile the parties, has her own share of misunderstanding. Because of her relationship with the Westmores and because she is a "foreign" woman, she is misunderstood by Alagarsami. The misunderstanding is cleared up when Alagarsami makes a trip in the company of Miss Summer to the lonely elephant hill. The old enmities and suspicions vanish during this meeting. A new chapter of understanding, friendship and love begins between Alagarsami and Miss Summer, the representatives of East and West.

In the third novel, *Men and Angels*, the argument about colonialism is extended to an investigation of the causes for its dissolution. Here again, the two cultures, American and Indian, are in close contact. In fact, the interaction extends to the more intimate domestic circle. Lucas Baber, the son of an American missionary, goes to India to investigate the mysterious circumstances of his father's reported death. He lives with the Indian family of the Chellappas and almost becomes a member of that family, assisting it in several ways. He falls in love with the English-educated daughter of the Chellappas, Sarojini, and meets her on the hill of Nagacoil. He even seeks the permission of her parents to marry her. The encounter between the East and the West in this novel, unlike the one in the previous novel, is from the beginning rooted in friendship and mutual understanding.

Thornton Baber, whose mysterious death in India brought Lucas to investigate it, is an intriguing figure. He is a subordinate missionary, stubborn over trivial things, short-sighted and indecisive over crucial ones. In his son's view, he is a "bumbling failure", incompetent, lonely in the midst of life, and something less than a human being. Thornton withdraws from the mission, goes native, dons an Indian *dhoti*, becomes an Indian citizen, and identifies himself with the Harijans and their cause. The Maravars, the traditional enemies of the Harijans, crucify him. Miss Nelson, a Eurasian friend of Thornton Baber, explains to the inquiring Lucas:

> In a sense he [Thornton] like colonialism, evangelical missions, and the whole business of the white man in India, was part of a last, fading, tattered remnant of a bygone age. He was firmly and inalterably a Victorian, a man committed to and entrenched in his absolutes. In everyday life, a failure in his devotion to principles and form and what not, he could unflinchingly lead, in the face of certain disaster, the charge of his light brigade. There is something foolish and something glorious about it. . . Don't praise him, don't scorn him, see him as he was, that as his death left you lost and alone, so the death of the Victorian era has left many young men like you, looking not so much for a real father as for some redefinition of life (White 1961:265).

Thornton Baber who, in the words of the author, is "synonymous with the Victorian era itself", has failed miserably in interpersonal relations while working in a different cultural environment.

The theme of interpersonal relations is a recurring one in several of the short stories in *Foreign Soil.* As the title of the book indicates, no soil need be foreign to anyone. Geographical and political divisions are losing their importance. White (1962: vii) says: "Indeed, there are no more unexplored rivers for our Huck Finns to travel down; there are only the cultural ones." The man-made differences of color, culture, geography, language, nation, race and religion are not, and cannot be, insurmountable barriers between people. No soil is native or foreign, but one's thinking may make it so. No soil can be deemed foreign when the emotions and needs of human beings are concerned. In White's cosmopolitan view, the only significant distinction is of sex. In his fiction, it is usually the attraction of the sexes—for instance, Miss Summer and Alagarsami, Lucas Baber and Sarojini—which builds bridges of understanding between people, transcending all other man-made differences. In his fiction, which was inspired by his live and extended contact with South India, White appears to subscribe to the view that mankind is one family, the whole world is one geographical entity, and man is the only worthwhile dimension.

NOTES AND REFERENCES

White, Robin. 1956. *House of Many Rooms*. New York: Harper.

__________ . 1959. *Elephant Hill*. New York: Harper.

__________ . 1961. *Men and Angels*. New York: Harper.

__________ . 1962. "Preface". *Foreign Soil: Tales of South India*. New York: Atheneum.

__________ . 1963. "Fiction in India". *The Reporter* 28:4:54-60.

9

The Revolutionary as Playwright: Dario Fo's Iconoclastic Art

Dario Fo, the Italian playwright who won the Nobel literature prize for 1997 is an out-and-out man of the theatre. He is an actor, dramatist, director and songwriter. Along with his actress wife Franca Rame, he has taken the Italian theatre by storm, as it were, and used it as an instrument to educate the masses on contemporary social and political issues. The play is the thing for Fo to raise the consciousness of the people on matters affecting their lives. He utilizes every trick of the dramatist's trade from the Middle Ages to the modern times to get across his message with great force. His dramatic career runs parallel to the history of Italy after World War II. Suzanne Cowan, writing in 1985, says that Fo's "work can only be understood as a continuous, uniquely creative response to the major social and political developments of the past thirty years."[1]

Dario Fo's involvement in the Italian theatre movement has several distinct phases. In the early phase, a period of apprenticeship, he acted and wrote humorous skits for the cabarets in Milan's well-known Piccolo Teatro. In the second phase he teamed up with his wife and presented a number of programmes on the Italian national radio and TV networks. His popularity soared to great heights with the TV show Canzonissima, which had an estimated viewership of twenty-five million, nearly half the population of Italy then. Fo was quite outspoken in his criticism of organized power-structures such as the Catholic hierarchy, bureaucracy, industrial bosses and the mafia. When the attacks on the establishment became more vigorous, the TV shows were censored. Fo took the cue and terminated his association with the mass media of entertainment.

The acting couple formed a theatre group, Campagna Dario Fo-Franca Rame, in 1958. Fo selected topical themes such as the Italian workers' movement and militant anarchy, wrote and produced a number of popular satirical comedies like *Gli Arcangeli non giacono a flipper* (1959, Archangels Don't Play Pinball) and *Aveva due pistole con gli ochhi bianchi e neri* (1960, He Had Two Pistols With White and Black Eyes).

The third phase begins with Fo and his wife joining Nuova Scena in 1968. This is a sort of cultural wing of the Italian Communist Party. This company initially gave Fo the freedom and flexibility he needed for his work. He experimented with new forms, materials and techniques. The most important Fo play staged under the auspices of Nuova Scena was *Mistero Buffo* (1969, Comic Mystery). It is an original work consisting of a series of monologues taken from medieval religious works. These materials are re-done and re-interpreted as social and political satire in Fo's popular play. The author makes use of popular culture, religious drama and parable, all of which go well with the masses, to show how the ruling ecclesiastical and noble hierarchies oppress the poor. No wonder the Vatican called it the "most blasphemous show in the history of television."[2] *Mistero Buffo* bears testimony to the painstaking research of Fo into the forms of popular theatre of the Middle Ages, including Commedia dell'arte, a form of low comedy. Two other important plays with political themes produced at Nuova Scena are: *Il funerale del padrone* (The Boss's Funeral) which deals with the daily sacrifice of factory hands, and *L'operatio conosce tercento parole, il padrone mille: per questo lui e il padrone* (The Worker Knows Three Hundred Words, The Boss a Thousand: That's Why He's The Boss). The second play is concerned with the role of culture and education in the class struggle. These plays were immensely popular with the new proletarian audience. Fo wrote a satire on the history of post-World War II Italy in the play entitled *Grande pantomima con bandiere e puppazi piccoli e medi* (1968). In this play, a beautiful woman representing capitalism is born out of a giant monster puppet, Communism. In some of these plays, Fo did not spare even the bureaucratic structure of the Communist Party. He found fault with the party's preference for reform and not for revolution. He broke his ties with Nuova Scena rather than compromise his beliefs.

The fourth phase begins with the establishment of Il Collectivo Teatrale La Commune in 1970. The aims of this company are "to raise the consciousness of the working classes, to encourage them to overthrow the bourgeois state, and to bring about a socialist government."[3] Under the banner of La Commune, Fo wrote several provocative plays on contemporary national and international political events. His best known play, *Morte accidentale di un anarchico* (1970, Accidental Death of an Anarchist) is a bold exposé of the police establishment. It deals with the death of Guiseppe Pinelli who allegedly committed suicide during a police interrogation in 1969. He was actually pushed out of a fourth-floor window by the police. The play is a savage attack on the brutality of the police and their stupid attempts to cover up the murder. The inquisitor in this play is a prankster with many names and disguises who lays bare the innumerable lies of the police. The play may appear loud, vulgar and scurrilous, but these are the elements of the medieval theatre. Fo says he uses farce because it gives "the possibility of going beyond character. You can comment on the situation while you're in it."[4] Farce is a device to separate the audience from the tragic issues discussed in the play.

Fo lampoons the police set-up in another play *Pum Pum Chi e? La Polizia!* (1972, Knock Knock, Who's There? The Police!) which is based on an actual incident. In 1969 Pietro Valpreda and two other anarchists were arrested on charges of planting bombs in a bank in downtown Milan. Fo traces the crime to the Prime Minister himself and calls it a "state massacre". Two other plays of this period focus on international events: *Fedayn* (1971) on the Palestinian problem and *Guerra di popolo Cile* (1973, People's War in Chile).

Just as Fo conducts his own research into medieval theatre for his forms, devices and techniques, so he meticulously delves into police records and investigative reports for his themes. His plays are fully documented; they are eloquent commentaries on Italian history and on social and political institutions. Fo is also in the habit of constantly revising and adding new political themes. Thus several scenes are re-located and the dialogue is often improvised. The actual performance of a play does not correspond with its printed version because of these continual revisions. Fo's plays also usually end with a discussion of the issues raised in them between the actors and the audience. The plays produced by La Commune depend for their appeal on the political debate and interaction with the audience because this company considers the theatre as a vehicle of militant cultural work and as a provider of counter-information. Thus Fo's La Commune is a meeting point between popular culture and radical intellectuals.

Although Fo is a strong advocate of proletarian revolution for the overthrow of the bourgeois state, yet he realized that his ideals are too revolutionary to be attained. So he switched over to a discussion of personal problems in the next phase. He says: "In the face of the failure of revolutionary ideals, the basic problem is how people relate to one another."[5] His plays in this period concentrate on male-female relationships. *Tutta casa, Letto e Chiesa* is a series of eight monologues, some serious, some amusing, but all focussing on the status of women in society. These are performed in England and the US *as One Woman Plays* (1981), *Female Parts* (1982) and *Escapes From the Zoo* (1983). *Orgasmo Adulto* exposes the condition of women in Italian society. The mothers and wives retaliate saying "we are all prisoners of the male organ." Another domestic comedy, *No se paga, No se paga!* (1974, We Won't Pay, We Won't Pay!) is a great success. It deals with a supermarket boycott by the housewives to protest high prices. Working class housewives steal large quantities of expensive food, try to conceal it from the detectives by stuffing it under their dresses and claiming pregnancy. This is an amusing satire on the police, bureaucracy, unions, welfare state and male privilege.

About Face is a commentary on the subjugation of the individual by the ruling class. It starts with the actual kidnapping of a former Prime Minister, Aldo Moro, and then turns into fantasy. The wealthy Agnelli is supposedly abducted by the Red Brigades. He is injured in a traffic accident, rescued by a Fiat worker, and mistaken for the rescuer. He undergoes plastic surgery and becomes the double of the rescuer. The shocking conclusion is that the wealthy man masterminded his own kidnapping.

In a recent interview Dario Fo says that he is only an actor, that too a jester. He says that the Swedish Academy has crowned the jester with the Nobel Prize. But in Fo's instance, jesting is a form of iconoclasm. In attempting to demolish the entrenched classes and established institutions, Fo is a social and political activist. What is the place of humour in plays with serious and revolutionary intent? Fo answered this question in 1971:

> What are those laughs that we put in there? We could take them out, if we wanted to. But they provide breathing space, to make the audience pay attention. An audience which isn't used to following a continuous discussion with no pauses, would grow bored after a while and lose its contact with the topic being discussed. So you invent comic solutions, special effects, grotesque situations. . . The problem is to adopt all means, the best there are, to arrive at the topic, which is what interests us.[6]

The dividing line between the revolutionary goal of social change and popular theatrical modes is pretty thin. A proletarian revolution is sought to be accomplished through the theatre which liberally employs the theatrical traditions of the Italian people for centuries. Fo's medium is therefore inseparable from his message.

NOTES AND REFERENCES

1. Quoted in "Dario Fo". *Contemporary Literary Criticism*. 32, Detroit: Gale Research Co., 1985. 171.
2. Celestine Bohlen and Rick Lyman. "Dario Fo: Italy's 'serious satirist'. *Frontline*. November 14, 1997. 91.
3. "Dario Fo". *Contemporary Literary Criticism*. 32, Detroit: Gale Research Co., 1985. 171.
4. Quoted in *Contemporary Literary Criticism*, 172.
5. Quoted in *Contemporary Literary Criticism*, 172.
6. Quoted in Suzanne Cowan, "The Throw Away Theatre of Dario Fo." *Drama Review* 19.2 (June 1975). 107.

10

The Hemingway Menagerie

> And the fear of you and the dread of you shall be upon every beast of the earth, and upon every fowl of the air, *upon* all that moveth upon the earth, and upon all the fishes of the sea; into your hand are they delivered.
>
> *Genesis, 9:2*

> Man is not much beside the great birds and beasts.
>
> Santiago in *The Old Man and the Sea.*

Even a cursory knowledge of the writings of Ernest Hemingway—both fiction and nonfiction—tells us that he was one of the few writers who were fascinated by the beasts of the earth, the birds of the air, and the fishes of the rivers and the seas. In fact, Hemingway did a little better than Noah because Noah did not seem to have bothered much about the insects. There is no specific mention of insects in God's command to Noah in the Book of Genesis. We are struck by the variety of wild life and domestic animals in Hemingway's works. From the common buffaloes to the exotic chamois, from large animals like elephants to small animals like cats and dogs, we come across almost all kinds of beasts in the Hemingway menagerie. The Hemingway canon is not merely a zoo, but an aquarium and an aviary as well. The variety of aquatic life throughout his works is amazing. From the trout and tuna to the marlin and the shark, from the sardines to the dolphin, we have plenty of watery creatures in the aquarium built into Hemingway's works. There is also an abundance of the fowl of the air. In his aviary we have canary, duck, eagle, flamingo, pelican, partridge, quail and so on. He also describes a great variety of insects in his writings. We can see ants, beetles, cockroaches, fleas, flies, grasshoppers, lice, locusts, mosquitoes, etc. The beasts, birds, fish and insects which we notice in the Hemingway world are from different countries and climates, from plains and mountains, from streams, lakes and oceans. It is difficult to come across such a great number and rich variety of creatures on earth, in water, and in the air in any other writer. What John Dryden said about the variety of Chaucer's characters—"Here is God's plenty"—may be said about the innumerable forms and species of life in Hemingway's works with greater justification. Fiction, as E.M. Forster reminds us, is about people, about human beings. And yet, Hemingway was able to smuggle in a whole lot of animals, fish, birds and insects into his fiction and make their presence relevant to the human condition.

What is more astonishing is that Hemingway displays an expert's knowledge of many of the beasts, birds, fish and insects. His *Death in the Afternoon* is a book on bulls and bullfighting comparable to Izaak Walton's *The Compleat Angler* and Herman Melville's cetelogical chapters in *Moby Dick* for its thoroughness and comprehensiveness. He describes the breeding, bravery, fighting qualities and even the love affairs of bulls in his book. His knowledge of wild life is attested by *Green Hills of Africa*, some African stories such as "The Short Happy Life of Francis Macomber," and a few reports from Tanganyika. His knowledge of aquatic life is equally sound. Izaak Walton's book on fishing is thorough, but it is limited to a study of fresh water fish and how to catch them. The internal evidence available in Hemingway's short stories like "Big Two-Hearted River," the novels, *The Sun Also Rises* and *The Old Man and the Sea*, and over half a dozen articles such as "The Best Rainbow Trout Fishing," "Tuna Fishing in Spain," "Fishing the Rhone Canal," Trout Fishing in Europe," "Marlin off the Morro," and "There She Breaches! or Moby Dick off the Morro," shows the range and thoroughness of his knowledge of angling not only fresh water fish, but salt water fish also. He talks with an expert's assurance on different types of bait for different kinds of fish. For instance, in his article, "The Best Rainbow Trout Fishing," he says:

> The rainbow takes the fly more willingly than he does the bait. The McGinty, a fly that looks like a yellow jacket, is the best. It should be tied on a number eight or ten hook (*By-Line*, 10).

In Hemingway's view rainbow trout fishing is "a rough, tough, mauling game, lacking in the meditative qualities of the Izaak Walton's school of angling" (*By-Line*, 8). He could have written a more complete book on angling than Walton's handbook published in 1653. Hemingway is the complete angler.

The proof of his expertise on birds is scattered throughout his work. His novel, *Across the River and Into the Trees*, is about duck shooting. He wrote an article on the carrion birds of Africa which he called "Wings Always Over Africa: An Ornithological Letter" (*By-Line*, 199). One of his short stories is entitled "A Canary for One." There are other birds such as flamingoes, pigeons, pheasants and warblers in his writings. He makes references to Bishop Stanley's *Familiar History of Birds* in his story "A Natural History of the Dead." His knowledge of birds is acquired through observation. In "Fathers and Sons," he describes an eagle catching its prey: [Nick] "remembering the time an eagle dropped through the whirling snow to strike a canvas covered decoy, rising, his wings beasts, the talons caught in the canvas" (594). His understanding of the birds and their ways is sufficient to qualify him as an ornithologist.

Hemingway observed various insects also with the same thoroughness which is a hallmark of his work. In his story "Now I Lay Me," Nick talks of a variety of insects, (beetles, grubs, wood ticks, angle-worms and grasshoppers) which he used as bait while fishing. In "A Way You'll Never Be," Nick gives a detailed description of locusts and how to catch them for using as bait. Then there is the well-known image of ants on a burning log of wood in *A Farewell to Arms*, but more of this later. These descriptions of various insects and their habits indicate the author's interest in entomology. What is noteworthy, however, is that his knowledge of the beasts, the birds, the fish and the insects is based on practical field observation and experience, and not on bookish knowledge alone. This is consistent with Hemingway's training as a journalist when he was asked to note down the observed facts. This is also in line with his own cardinal principle in writing, namely, describing "the real thing" or "what happened in action."

After noting Hemingway's unusual – unusual for a creative writer – interest in animals of all kinds, his expertise in bullfighting, piscatology and wild life, and his deep interest in ornithology and entomology, one may ask what use he had made of it in his creative writing. What is the relevance of animals in his scheme of things? What place do they have in his worldview? He uses a number of metaphors, images and symbols related to animals. For instance, he sees the bullfight as an appropriate metaphor for the human predicament as he understood it. So he made a thorough study of all aspects of the bullfight. Man is encircled like the bull, tormented like him, and is killed in the end like the bull. His strength and bravery are of little avail in the face of forces beyond his control. There is no satisfactory explanation for the death of the bull whose strength and bravery are far superior to the torero's. Like Santiago's marlin, the bull is killed through "trickery." In a similar way, the reason for the death, literal or symbolic, of many of Hemingway's characters remains a mystery. Such death or injury can only be taken as part of life, as the way of the modern world.

Indeed, Hemingway seems to look upon the world as an extensive bullring where death is a firm certainty for all and violent injury a dangerous possibility for many. The same sort of violence may be seen in hunting or fishing. The animal or fish is relentlessly pursued, cornered or hooked, and killed. Santiago's rationalization that "everything kills everything else in some way" (*The Old Man*, 117) is perhaps the novelist's own insight into the nature of life. There may be design in this maintenance of a balance among various forms of life, but killing, as Hemingway sees it, seems to follow no recognizable law. Hence his characters seek a spiritual and emotional antidote to senseless and disorderly killing in the ritual killing. In the bullring, the matador deliberately confronts death by risking his life before an enraged bull. The rules and conventions of the bullfight impose a certain order, discipline, and grace not available on the battlefield. Though it is "the only art in which the artist is in danger of death and in which the degree of brilliance is left to the fighter's honour" (*Death in the Afternoon*, 91), yet the matador can create, enhance, and control that danger to his advantage. The bullfight teaches him the virtue of "grace under pressure" without which life in Hemingway's violent world is almost impossible. By his orderly and disciplined conduct in the presence of danger, that is, "grace under pressure," he also learns to disregard the consequence completely as he encounters the bull with the muleta and the sword. When he kills the bull by thrusting the sword between his shoulder blades, he assumes the "Godlike attribute" of giving death. At the "moment of truth," he imaginatively identifies himself with the dying bull, merges with him by becoming "one figure" joined by the sword, and in this process he vicariously experiences death. This purges the feeling of mortality in him and he momentarily feels immortal. That is, in assuming the "Godlike attribute" he overmasters the vagaries of chance for the moment. Thus bullfighting acquires a mythic or ritualistic dimension and enables its participants to escape from the world of irrational violence to a world of controlled violence. It makes the participant, and by extension the observer, a master, rather than a victim, of death. The same kind of immersion is possible in other forms of ritual like fishing, hunting and sexual intercourse which, in Hemingway's view, are analogous to bullfighting. When Nick Adams goes to fish the Big Two-Hearted River, or Jake Barnes participates in the fiesta at Pamplona, or Hemingway himself goes on an African safari, they are seeking means of escaping the violence and terror of the world through these ritual-filled activities.

Hemingway's characters like Nick Adams and Jake Barnes who are victims of a psychic injury, believe that ritual activity, real or vicarious, provides life, light, order and cleanliness in the midst of death, darkness, disorder and dirt. In the bullfight, there is life in the midst of death, a feeling of immortality as death is administered to the bull.

The bullfight, as Hemingway describes it, is a well-ordered, well-disciplined act of ritual which has a profound therapeutic effect on the matador and on the spectators. In his view, other forms of ritual like fishing and hunting have also identical possibilities. The shell-shocked Nick in "Now I Lay Me" attempts to drive away his nightly fears by vicarious fishing, and if he cannot fish, he says his prayers over and over again for all the people he has known. Fishing and prayer are interchangeable means of driving out darkness and death for him. Bullrings, trout streams, East African jungles and clean cafés are oases in the chaotic and endless desert that is the modern world.

All the activities which deeply interested Hemingway—bullfighting, hunting, fishing—are means of releasing tensions, fears and hatreds. This release makes a man feel better, and this is what the wounded or shocked Hemingway settles for. He describes the bullfight as a three-act tragedy complete with the traditional catharsis. It is

> The faena that takes a man out of himself and makes him feel immortal while it is proceeding, that gives him an ecstasy; that is, while momentary, as profound as any religious ecstasy; moving all the people together and increasing in emotional intensity as it proceeds, carrying the bullfighter with it. . . and being moved as it responds in a growing ecstasy of ordered, formal, passionate, increasing disregard for death that leaves you, when it is over and the death administered to the animal that has made it possible, as empty, as changed, and as sad as any major emotion will leave you (*Death in the Afternoon*, 206-207).

A similar catharsis is possible through fishing, hunting and killing which are virtually interchangeable for him. Jake's fishing trip with his friend, Bill Gorton, to Burguete and his absorbing interest in the bullfight at Pamplona—he is an *aficionado*—not only enable him to drive out his despair, but, one may venture to suggest, offer a sexual cripple like him vicarious sexual gratification. Pablo gets rid of animal passions by his brutal killing of the Fascists. He could sleep "like a baby" because, as Pilar observes, his condition was comparable to the bullfighter's after the corrida.

The killing of a Kenyan buffalo makes Hemingway feel "a sort of elation" and a "little quiet inside" (*Green Hills of Africa*, 120). Anselmo experiences an elation whenever he hunts. Francis Macomber feels "a wild unreasonable happiness" after shooting a buffalo. He is purged of fear and he feels "absolutely different" (*Short Stories*, 32). By deliberately confronting the beasts, the fish and the birds, Hemingway and his heroes seek a release of the harmful emotions so they can feel better again. The pursuit of happiness which is an ideal enshrined in the American constitution is possible through the bullfight and similar activities. These activities involve man's direct involvement with the beasts, birds and fish. When Pedro Romero confronts the bull in the ring, when Santiago pursues the marlin on the high seas, or when Hemingway goes big-game hunting in Kenya, man and beast are face to face. Santiago observes, "man is not much beside the great birds and beasts" (*Old Man*, 68). Actually, it is an uneven contest. Yet man is able to subdue the beast through his cunning and weapons.

The bull in the ring is a trapped animal. The hooked fish and the caged bird are also trapped. This is a recurring image in Hemingway's fiction. The human condition, as he seems to imply, is no better. Jake is trapped by his funny wound; Catherine is trapped by her narrow hips; her baby is trapped in the womb; Frederic Henry is trapped by circumstances; El Sordo is trapped on the hill. Man is as helpless as the ensnared animal. His trickery which enables him to control or kill wild animals is of little use when he is himself trapped. This feeling of the helplessness of man is brought out by the author in a vivid image in *A Farewell to Arms*. Frederic Henry muses over the death of his baby and recalls an earlier incident when he had put a log full of ants on top of the fire. The ants went towards the centre, that is where the fire was. Then they turned back and ran towards the end and fell off into the fire. Whichever way they moved, the fire caught up with them. Instead of taking out the log from the fire and saving the ants in time, Henry threw a cup of water on the burning log. This only steamed the ants. Henry's predicament in Switzerland, and by extension, the human condition, is comparable to that of the ants on the burning log of wood. Man is hopelessly and helplessly trapped. There is no escape for him just as there is none for the ants or other animals.

Another image is that of the "flayed rabbit." Henry likens Catherine's freshly born baby to a skinned rabbit. Robert Jordan frequently refers to Maria as rabbit. After she was mass-raped and her head was shaved by the Fascists, she looked very much like a flayed rabbit. Fascist Spain, by implication, is like a flayed rabbit.

Among the domestic animals, the cat figures frequently in Hemingway's work. A big loving cat named F. Puss was actually used as a baby-sitter for Hemingway's son, Bumby, in Paris. One of his stories is entitled "Cat in the Rain." Here a young wife yearns for fun and domestic happiness against the background of a dull life in a hotel with a husband who is unimaginative and unresponsive. The woman identifies her own love of a few good things of life with the possession of a cat she sees in the rain outside. Thus the cat symbolises for her a modicum of happiness and enjoyment. The qualities which the writer associates with a cat in his other stories are quietness, playfulness, resilience and self-sufficiency.

In "A Canary for One," again a domestic pet is used. An American lady convinced herself that American men make the best husbands. She prevents her daughter marrying a Swiss. She takes a songbird, a canary from Palermo, as a gift to her daughter. She asserts that American men make the best husbands before an American couple who are about to separate.

We have seen that Hemingway is equally knowledgeable about the African wild animals, the enraged Spanish bulls, the giant Cuban marlins, the big Italian cats, and the singing Palermo canaries. Other American writers such as Herman Melville, Marianne Moore and Sylvia Plath have also written about various animals. But not many writers have dealt with such a variety of beasts, birds, fish and insects, and that with the same degree of expertise.

Hemingway loved animals and lived with them. He understood more clearly than many others the relationship of man to other creatures. His concern for ecological harmony is similar to Thoreau's. Jake and Bill escape to Burguete for a quiet communion with nature. The rituals involved in bullfighting are a stylized representation of man's organic relationship to nature. Hemingway laments the pillaging and plundering of the virgin lands of Africa:

> A continent ages quickly once we come. The natives live in harmony with it. . ..A country wears out quickly unless man puts back in it all his residue and that of all his beasts. When he quits using beasts and uses machines, the earth defeats him quickly. The machine can't reproduce, nor does it fertilise the soil (*Green Hills of Africa*, 236).

Hemingway feels that the dream of America as a new Garden of Eden was effectively and permanently shattered by the reality of America as an industrial giant polluting the good earth. The machine has undone the garden. The desire to preserve a spontaneous, organic and traditional relationship between man and nature is quite strong in Hemingway. He protested in vain against the desecration of the sacred tie between man and nature like many of his illustrious predecessors such as Thoreau, Melville, Whitman and Mark Twain. Hemingway's works are in a sense a modern Noah's ark.

WORKS CITED

Dryden, John. *Preface to Fables*. Ed. C.T. Thomas. (Macmillan Annotated Classics). Madras: Macmillan, 1977.

Forster, E.M. *Aspects of the Novel*. New York: Harcourt, 1954. [1927].

Hemingway, Ernest. *Across the River and Into the Trees*. New York: Scribner's 1950.

__________. *By-Line*. New York: Bantam Books, 1968.

__________. *Death in the Afternoon*. New York: Scribner's, 1932.

__________. *A Farewell to Arms*. New York: Scribner's, 1929.

__________. *For Whom the Bell Tolls*. New York: Scribner's, 1940.

__________. *Green Hills of Africa*. New York: Scribner's, 1935.

__________. *The Old Man and the Sea*. New York: Scribner's, 1952.

__________. *The Sun Also Rises*. New York: Scribner's, 1928.

__________. *The Short Stories*. New York: Scribner's, 1955.

11

English Language Teaching in the Twenty-first Century

English Language Teaching (ELT) methodology has been changing almost every twenty years. These changes are based on a variety of factors such as the aims of the learners, the prevailing psychological theories of learning, the linguistic theories current, and the advances and innovations in technology. The Grammar-Translation Method, the Direct Method, the Bilingual Method, the Graded Method, the Language Control Method, the Linguistic Method and Communicative Language Teaching are some of the methods that have been widely used in the twentieth century in different parts of the world. Each method is developed to meet the new demands of and emerging challenges from learners. Every method attempts to absorb the prevailing beliefs regarding the learning process and the nature of language. Also, new developments in technology are quickly utilised in the service of language instruction to make it more interesting and efficient.

For instance, we may recall the use of phonograph records, radio, film strips, tape recorders, language laboratories, audio and video cassettes and television for enriching the learning experience of students. The use of one or more of these gadgets by particular individuals or institutions depended on their affluence and their adaptability to technological changes. The methods listed above are all useful and valid. They are reasonably successful in achieving their specific goals.

The situation in ELT is changing once again, perhaps more rapidly than ever. There is an increasing demand for learning English owing to political changes, economic opportunities, social demands, professional needs, and, more importantly, the Information Technology Revolution which is sweeping the world with the force of a hurricane. In the circumstances, academic life and English Language Teaching methodology cannot remain unaffected.

One paradoxical fact is that against 350 million native speakers of English, there are 1,500 million users of English today. Perhaps no other language is spoken and/or used by such a large number of people. Both the native speakers and users of English are spread all over the world making English a global language in a very real sense. There are certain areas such as civil aviation where English is the only language used throughout the world.

The aims of teaching and of learning English language have been changing fast. The emphasis is shifting from a study of English literature to the acquisition of language skills. Utilitarian considerations prevail over cultural factors demanding acquisition or improvement of communication skills which include a whole range of oral and written sub-skills. Universities and colleges continue to teach largely literature-oriented courses and the syllabi are repetitive and far from relevant to the changing situation. The expanding opportunities for teaching English are quickly seized by private institutes which often do not have qualified and trained faculty, and adequate infrastructure and equipment.

There is a great demand for need-based courses which are also called English for Specific (or Special) Purposes (ESP). The current revolution in Information Technology is both a challenge and an opportunity for ELT. It has been mankind's recurring experience that the more efficient systems prevail over the less efficient ones. So it will be with the adaptation of Information Technology to English Language Teaching methodology.

R.L. Chartrand and J.W. Morentz define Information Technology in the following terms:

> Information Technology means collection, storage, processing, dissemination, and use of information. It is not confined to hardware and software, but acknowledges the importance of

> man and the goals he sets for this technology, the values he employed in making these choices, the assessment criteria used to decide whether he is controlling the technology and is being enriched by it (121).

The use of the computer in language instruction is no longer a passing fad, but an irresistible trend. Micro-computers have accelerated the pace of change in ELT methodology by providing interactive and individualised learning. They can be linked to other media; they can be utilised for a variety of software such as audio devices, touch screens, etc. The Computer Assisted (or Aided) Language Learning (CALL) is transforming the concept of the classroom, the ELT methodology, the role of the teacher and several related matters. For instance, it is no longer necessary for the students to meet in a traditional classroom at a specified time and listen to a teacher. The students may be scattered over a large area and sit in front of their computers and press a few keys to learn their lessons. Computers facilitate distance education by providing it to large numbers of students, and at times and places convenient to them. Computer networks also provide communication among students without the teacher's intervention.

The students using computers can work or learn at their own pace. A course through computers makes the student more actively involved in the learning process. He will have more fun learning and learning through his own efforts. As Martin Phillips observes: "The computer offers a tool to students which allows them to assume mastery of their own learning experience." (Leech, 7)

The impact of computers on teaching materials is also significant. Instead of being fixed, they can be modified to suit the needs of individual students. The teaching methodology has been revolutionized with the introduction of computers. For instance, the visual impact of graphics used in CALL can be purposeful and interesting.

Computer cannot replace the teacher, but he will have a rather different role than the one he has been playing hitherto. He may programme the materials and supplement them whenever necessary. It is the teacher, not the technology, who should have the power to make decisions. The areas of human and mechanical action and the roles of man and machine in the growing educational enterprise should be clearly demarcated. With the introduction of the computer as a powerful teaching device, a new balance between the computer, the teaching materials and the teacher has to be struck.

The advantages of CALL are many. It promotes interactive learning because the learner transmits a message and receives one in return. It involves the students personally and emotionally to a greater degree than a printed text can. It provides immediate feedback; the mistakes in learning are notified immediately. The mistakes are pointed out and explained. The learner is guided towards the correct answer. Congratulatory messages for right answers flash on the screen to encourage the student. Another advantage of CALL is individualised instruction which is sometimes known as flexistudy (flexible study). In this type of learning, each student learns at his own pace; slow learners need not feel they are rushed and fast learners need not feel bored with the slow pace of activity. The learner can choose from a variety of programmes to suit his ability and interests. CALL is learner-centred unlike several traditional modes of learning and teaching. It takes into account the learner's strengths, weaknesses and problems and it is geared to the learner's specific needs. Yet another great advantage of CALL is its outreach. It can be used and used effectively even in such places as hospitals, prisons and offices which are generally considered not conducive to learning.

Word Processor which is a product of Information Technology is a useful tool for teaching writing. It helps in different stages of writing such as pre-writing, writing, revising and editing. The computer can have multiple functions: it can be a tutor, a partner in language games, a guide, a reference book, and a generator of examples.

Language teachers have been making use of the developments in technology. They realise the power of teaching language through various media to explain meanings, to reinforce memory, and to reduce boredom. CALL combines in itself both audio and visual materials and it excites the curiosity of the learners much more than other devices used till now in language teaching.

Francis Bacon who was hailed as the wisest and the brightest of mankind by Alexander Pope, said nearly four hundred years ago, in his "Of Heresies": "Knowledge itself is power." In his *Novum Organum* I, he elaborated this dictum: "Knowledge and human power are synonymous since the ignorance of the cause frustrates the effect." We need to modify Bacon's aphorism to suit the modern context to: "Information itself is power." The visionary poet, William Blake, wrote more than a century ago in his "Auguries of Innocence":

To see a World in a Grain of Sand
And Heaven in a Wild Flower
Hold infinity in the Palm of your hand
And Eternity in an hour.

The "Grain of Sand" which can reveal a whole new world seems to be the silicon chip.

NOTE

The three terms, information, knowledge and wisdom, are defined in *Webster's New World Dictionary of the American Language* (College Edition) (1960) in the following way: *Information* applies to facts that are gathered in any way, as by reading, observation, hearsay, etc., and does not necessarily connote validity. *Knowledge* applies to any body of facts gathered by study, observation, etc., and to the ideas inferred from these facts, and connotes an understanding of what is known. *Wisdom* implies superior judgement and understanding based on broad knowledge.

WORKS CITED

Chartrand, R.L. and J.W. Morentz (1979), *I.T. and Serving Society*, London: Pergamon.

Phillips, Martin (1986), "CALL in its Educational Context." Leech, Geoffrey and Christopher N. Candlin (eds.) 1986, *Computers in English Language Teaching and Research*. London: Longman.

12

John Keats as a Literary Critic

John Keats's aesthetic theories have received considerable critical attention, but his contribution to literary criticism has not been, it seems to me, fully assessed. He has expressed his views not only on poetry, but on many major writers, including Shakespeare, Milton and Wordsworth, without inhibitions. He may not have written critical essays on any writer, but his observations are scattered throughout his letters and a few poems. This paper is an attempt to examine Keats's critical remarks on writers in some detail. Such a review may enable us to understand his critical methods, principles and values.

Let us now consider his observations on some great writers. In his poem, "To Homer," he says that the Greek poet was endowed with a "triple sight" to see Earth, Heaven and Hell; blindness is no handicap to a poet blessed with a rich imagination. In his poem, "The Poet," he expresses a similar view that a poet sees beyond "where Learning hath no light." He learnt Italian for reading Dante which is "well worth the while" (156)*. Keats has preferred the Elizabethans to the contemporaries because their grandeur and merit are "uncontaminated and unobtrusive." They are like the roses and eagles while the moderns are like pricks and owls (44).

Keats makes four perceptive comments on Shakespeare: (1) intensity of art, (2) negative capability, (3) life of allegory, and (4) a fine writer is the most genuine Being. Let us consider these briefly. He compares Benjamin West's painting, "Death on the Pale Horse," with Shakespeare's *King Lear* and says that West's picture lacks intensity: "the excellence of Art is its intensity, capable of making all disagreeables evaporate, from their being in close relationship with Beauty & Truth" (32). *King Lear* has that intensity. In the same letter he states that Shakespeare possessed "Negative Capability" which distinguishes a Man of Achievement from others. He explains this term: "when man is capable of being in uncertainties, Mysteries, doubts, without any irritable reaching after fact & reason. . . with a great poet the sense of Beauty overcomes every other consideration" (32). Coleridge, in spite of the wide range of his intellectual interests, did not possess this quality. The third comment, "Shakespeare led a life of Allegory: his works are the comments on it" is explained by Keats by saying that the mystery of a

* The numbers in parentheses refer to the numbers of Keats's letters.

man's life of any worth cannot be easily understood. It is figurative like the scriptures. To clarify this point, Keats compares Shakespeare with Byron and says that the latter is "not figurative." This remark epitomizes the variety, profundity and mystery of Shakespeare. In yet another observation, Keats states that "a fine writer is the most genuine Being in the World. Shakespeare and the paradise lost every day become greater wonders to me" (142). Shakespeare's works and Milton's *Paradise Lost* are examples of fine writing and hence these poets are the most genuine Beings.

Keats does not allow his admiration for *Paradise Lost* which he describes as the "most remarkable Production in the World" (156) to cloud his judgement on Milton. Although he loves fine phrases and although he is astonished at the capacity of a northern language like English to be a worthy substitute for classical languages like Latin and Greek in the composition of an epic, he hates Miltonic inversions. He complains that Paradise Lost "is a corruption of our Language" (156). He considers Chatterton "the purest writer in the English Language" (151); he prefers "the native music of English to Milton's diction. "I have but lately stood on my guard against Milton. Life to him would be death to me. Miltonic verse cannot be written but it [in] the vein of art" (156). Keats's preference for English words is not born of any jingoism because he is proficient in several European Languages and he knows their relative strengths. For instance, he readily concedes the music inherent in Italian (19). He has first-hand knowledge of Latin as he had attempted *Hyperion* in the grand style of Milton. He makes an interesting comparison between Milton and Wordsworth on their concern for humanity. He says that in "Tintern Abbey," Wordsworth's genius explores the "burden of the Mystery." "He is a Genius and superior [to] us, in so far as he can, more than we, make discoveries, and shed a light in them – Here I must think Wordsworth is deeper than Milton" (64). Then follows a critical analysis of the growth of human knowledge in the two centuries between Milton and Wordsworth: "There is really a grand march of intellect. It proves that a mighty providence subdues the mightiest Minds to the service of the time being, whether it be in human knowledge or Religion" (64). It is no reflection on Milton's power as a philosopher if he did not "think into the human heart, as Wordsworth has done" (64). He was content with hinting at good and evil in *Paradise Lost*. The reformation influenced Milton and he was content to present ideas on virtue, vice and chastity in *Comus*.

Although Keats thinks that Wordsworth was a greater philosopher than Milton, he is skeptical about the place of philosophy in poetry. He asks:

> for the sake of a few fine imaginative or domestic passages, are we to be bullied into a certain Philosophy engendered in the whims of an

> Egotist. . . We hate poetry that has a palpable design on us. . . Poetry should be great and unobtrusive, a thing which enters into one's soul, and does not startle it or amaze it with itself but with its subject (44).

In another significant observation, he distinguishes "the Wordsworthian or egotistical sublime" from the "Poetical character." He argues that a poet has no identity; he is a chameleon who has the same delight in creating an Iago as in creating an Imogen (93). Keats rates *The Excursion* as "one of the three things superior in the modern world" (37). He is aware of Wordsworth's "egotism, Vanity, and bigotry"; he is fair in his assessment of Wordsworth as "a great poet if not a philosopher" (50).

The same unfailing objectivity may be seen in Keats's observations on Lord Byron. He calls Byron and Scott "the two literary kings" of his time. He calls Byron "a fine thing" in the sphere of "the worldly theatrical, and pantomimical." But, unlike Shakespeare, Byron is not figurative; his is not a life of allegory. In another letter, Keats compares Byron with himself: "There is this great difference between us. He describes what he sees—I describe what I imagine. Mine is the hardest task" (156). The difference is between realistic description and imaginative description. The latter type obviously requires greater creativity.

Keats's personal modesty and intellectual honesty may be seen in his remarks on Shelley. He is aware of Shelley's weaknesses and points them out clearly, but politely:

> There is only part of it [*The Cenci*] I am judge of, the Poetry and dramatic effect. . . *an artist* . . .must have 'self concentration' selfishness perhaps. You I am sure will forgive me for sincerely remarking that you might curb your magnanimity and be more of an artist, and 'load every rift' of your subject with ore. The thought of such discipline must fall like cold chains upon you, who perhaps never sat with your wings furl'd for six Months together (227).

He admits his own deficiencies in his earlier work, *Endymion*, and hence he feels his advice to Shelley might sound "extraordinary" (227).

Keats is critical of his own work:

> My own domestic criticism has given me pain without comparison beyond what Blackwood or the Quarterly could possibly inflict... J.S. is perfectly right in regard to the slip-shod Endymion. . . It is as good as I had power to make it—by myself—had I been nervous about its being a perfect piece, & with that view asked advice, & trembled over every page, it would not have been written; for it is not in my nature to fumble. . . I have written independently *without Judgment*. I may write independently & *with*

> *Judgment* hereafter. The Genius of Poetry must work out its own salvation in a man: It cannot be matured by law and precept; but by sensation & watchfulness in itself. That which is creative must create itself—In Endymion, I leaped headlong into the Sea. . . . I was never afraid of failure, for I would sooner fail than not be among the greatest (90).

This is not a defence of his failure, but an admission of it and a strong resolve to learn from failure and improve and excel. It requires clarity of mind to realize one's faults and courage to admit them. It is only those who are strong in mind who can do these.

He does not spare even Leigh Hunt who was his closest friend at the start of his career. He is forthright on Hunt:

> He understands many a beautiful thing; but then instead of other minds giving credit to the same degree of perception as he himself possesses—he begins an explanation in such a curious manner that our taste and self-love is offended continually. Hunt does one harm by making fine things pretty and beautiful things hateful (98).

Keats's critical methods are analysis and comparison, the same which T.S. Eliot advocated much later. The difference between Elizabethan and contemporary writers is analyzed threadbare.

Similarly, the reasons for the superior philosophy of Wordsworth are clinically analyzed. Comparison as a critical tool is used by Keats for clarifying his points. Shakespeare and Coleridge, Shakespeare and Byron, Milton and Chatterton, Milton and Wordsworth are compared for explaining his ideas. Keats judges writers by the highest standards and gives praise where it is due; he does not hesitate to condemn something when it is not good; he does not allow any personal considerations to weigh in his critical judgment. He applies the same severe tests to his own work. The only writer whom Keats praises without reservations is Shakespeare. In fact, Shakespeare becomes an ideal standard by which other writers are evaluated. As a literary critic, Keats shows intellectual honesty and courageous expression. He could afford to do that because he loved "the principle of beauty in all things" (186) and because his first and last loyalty was to poetry.

WORKS CITED

The Complete Poetry and Selected Prose of John Keats. Ed. Harold Edgar Briggs. New York: The Modern Library, 1951.

The Letters of John Keats. Ed. Maurice Buxton Forman. Fourth Edition. London: Oxford University Press, 1952.

13

Huckleberry Finn's Adventures with Women

One of the significant lacunae in the available criticism on *Adventures of Huckleberry Finn* seems to concern the role of the women characters in shaping the attitudes and in triggering the actions of the boy-hero of the novel. In the past fifteen years or more, there have been three books and a few articles on the women in Mark Twain's life and in his fiction. Peter Stoneley's book *Mark Twain and the Feminine Aesthetic* is concerned more with the larger question of the elements which constitute Mark Twain's "feminine aesthetic" than with the impact of the women characters on Huckleberry Finn in his impressionable years. Stoneley finds a dichotomy between Samuel Clemens the man and Mark Twain the mask, between his private preferences and his public posturings. Resa Willis's book, *Mark and Livy: The Love Story of Mark Twain and the Woman Who Almost Tamed Him*, deals with the relationship of Mark Twain and his wife. The third book, Skandera-Trombley's *Mark Twain in the Company of Women*, has also little to say on this question. Of the articles on the broad theme of women and Mark Twain, Trygve Thoresen's piece "'Virtuous According to Their Lights': Mark Twain's Early Work," is exclusively devoted to a study of the treatment of women in Mark Twain's early newspaper writings. John Daniel Stahl's article, "Mark Twain and Female Power: Public and Private," describes an amusing experience on the statue of Queen Elizabeth I of England. Regina Stein and Robert Lidston's essay, "The Mother Figure in Twain's Mississippi Novels," suggests that Twain's mother, Jane Clemens, is the model for several of the women in his fiction. She is "prematurely old, outspoken, occasionally severe, but big-hearted." Jami Parkison's paper, "A Woman's Mark Twain," considers women characters in the entire range of his fictional concerns. Pascal Covici Jr.'s "Mark Twain and the Feminine" is a review of some of the recent books on the subject. My paper proposes to explore in some detail Huckleberry Finn's relationship with the women he meets in the course of his "adventures" and how these women, wittingly or unwittingly, mould his character and direct the course of his actions.

Huckleberry Finn lives with four families where women dominate or take care of him. His stay with these families ranges from many months in the case of the Widow Douglas, to several weeks in the case of the Phelpses, a few days in the case of the Grangerfords and the Wilkses. He also makes a short visit to St.Petersburg to find out from Mrs. Judith Loftus what was happening in the neighbourhood after the disappearance of Huck and Jim. All these are Southern white women. There are a few black women with the Grangerfords, the Wilkses and the Phelpses, but Huck has hardly any interaction with them.

Huck's first adventure in the world of women is with the Widow Douglas who took him "for her son" and she wanted to "sivilize" him. He does not like her methods of "sivilizing" him: "it was rough living in the house all the time, considering how dismal regular and decent the widow was in all her ways; and so when I couldn't stand it no longer, I lit out"(7). Huck enjoys the freedom of the outdoors but not the discipline of a household presided over by the Widow Douglas. But he had to go back to her to earn respectability and thereby qualify to join Tom's band of robbers. Once again, he had to exchange his "old rags" for "the new clothes" which "cramped" him up. The widow is a pious disciplinarian. She has fixed timings for meals and she offers grace before supper. That is too much for the carefree Huck. The widow's care for her charge extends to teaching him the Bible. As a pragmatist, Huck is not interested in the story of Moses when he learns that he was dead a long time ago. The widow prevents Huck smoking saying that it was "a mean practice and wasn't clean." Huck finds fault with her for bothering about Moses who was "no use to anybody" and not allowing him to smoke which he thinks has "some good in it." Huck also faults her on her double standards in asking him not to smoke, but she herself takes snuff which is just another product of tobacco. The widow is a typical symbol of religious piety, discipline, respectability and cleanliness, but her dual standards expose her hypocrisy. Her efforts to reform and "sivilize" Huck are, of course, well-meaning.

Her sister, Miss Watson, is a sterner disciplinarian and less tolerant of Huck's manners, or lack of them. Huck's fidgety movements are all disapproved by her and she promptly corrects him. When he could not take it any more, he just wants to go away somewhere, even if it was "a bad place"; he wouldn't like to go to the "good place' because Miss Watson wants to go there herself. Miss Watson's idea of entry into the good place is through singing on a harp all day long forever and ever.

Coming from the same family, the two sisters have many things in common. Both are deeply religious; both believe in the efficacy of prayer; both are stern disciplinarians, both of them have the urge to reform and mother an orphan like Huck. Huck's experience is that the widow is more tolerant, understanding and kind than Miss Watson. He compares the two sisters:

> Sometimes the widow would take me on one side and talk about Providence in a way to make a boy's mouth water; but maybe next day Miss

> Watson would take hold and knock it all down again. I judged I could see that there was two Providences, and a poor chap would stand considerable show with the widow's Providence; but if Miss Watson got him there warn't no help for him any more (15).

Another telling illustration of the temperaments of the two sisters is the way they react to Huck's questions on prayer. When Huck complains that he prayed three or four times for hook for his fish-line without success, Miss Watson simply brushes him aside saying he is a fool. But the widow patiently explains to Huck that one can get "spiritual gifts" through prayer. She urges him to do selfless service.

When Huck is about to be disqualified from joining Tom's band of robbers because he does not have a family, Huck offers Miss Watson for killing if necessary. This shows how much he despises her. After spending three or four months with the widow, Huck gets used to her ways. On her part, the widow appreciates his progress to "sivilization": "The widow said I was coming along slow but sure, and doing very satisfactory. She said she warn't ashamed of me" (18). With a genuine maternal concern for Huck's safety, she joins the judge in getting Huck out of Pap's control and later tries to release him from the hut where Pap locks him up.

These pious, harsh and humourless women strengthen, although unwittingly, Huck's resolve to go out and enjoy the freedom of the outdoors. If civilization meant all manner of restrictions on his movements, habits and behaviour as the two sisters seemed to believe, Huck would have none of it. At the same time, Huck's thinking is influenced by the widow's preachings. When he tries to help the bandits on board the *Walter Scott* by sending a ferry to rescue them, he thinks the widow would be proud of him for that: "I judged she would be proud of me for helping these rapscallions, because rapscallions and dead beats is the kind the widow and good people takes the most interest in" (63).

Huck's next adventure is his visit with Mrs. Judith Loftus in St. Petersburg. This is in a sense a misadventure because the shrewd Mrs. Loftus finds out through clever strategems the sex of her nocturnal visitor. But Huck is able to get important information that her husband would search Jackson's Island after midnight for the runaway nigger and claim the reward money of three hundred dollars. Huck rushes back to Jim and alerts him: "Git up and hump yourself, Jim! There ain't a minute to lose. They're after us" (53). This chance meeting with Mrs. Loftus and her garrulity trigger Huck's voyage down the river with Jim. At that time it was only an instinctive and panic reaction to escape the search without any plans or a clear destination.

The third family which Huck encounters on his voyage is that of the Grangerfords. While the head of the family, Saul, and the other men wanted to make sure that Huck is not a Shepherdson and that he does not carry arms, it is Rachel Grangerford who, with a maternal instinct, observes that he is all wet and presumably hungry. She immediately arranges for dry clothes and some food. The biblical name, Rachel, who weeps for her lost children, is significant here because Mrs. Grangerford also lost three of her sons in the senseless feud with the Shepherdsons. Huck admires Col. Grangerford as a gentleman. He remembers that the Widow Douglas had said that to be well-born is worth in a man as in a horse. The widow herself belongs to the first aristocracy in his town. Here also Huck's opinion is shaped by the widow's comments.

In the Grangerford family, Huck meets young girls for the first time in his voyage. He admires the sentimental pictures and poems of Emmeline Grangerford who died at the age of fifteen. Miss Charlotte, aged twenty-three, is "tall and proud and grand. . . . She was beautiful" (87). Her sister Sophia, aged twenty, although different, is "gentle and sweet, like a dove" (87). Huck's role in fetching Sophia's Testament in which her rendezvous with her lover, Harney Shepherdson, is intimated, leads to her elopement and the consequent fierce battle in which many of both the families are killed. Huck feels guilty of this massacre because he thinks he is responsible for Sophia's elopement. If only he had informed her father in time, the Colonel would have locked her up and "this awful mess" would not have occurred. The tragic killings stemming from Sophia's elopement hasten Huck's departure.

If Huck's fortuitous visit with the Grangerfords gives him an exposure to the southern aristocratic women, old and young, his visit to the Wilks home, which is again a chance meeting, provides him an opportunity to interact with three teenage girls, Mary Jane, Susan and Joanna. Mary Jane is red-headed; "she was the most awful beautiful" (130). Huck is impressed with the manner in which the two older sisters prevail on Joanna to apologize to him when she refuses to swallow all his "stretchers" on his life in England. Mary Jane's innocence can be seen in her face. Huck observes to her: "I don't want no better book than your face is. A body can set down and read it off like coarse print" (149). Later on, he comments: "She had the grit to pray for Judus if she took the notion – there warn't no backdown to her" (151). The courteous and cultured behaviour of these sisters, their innocence and their gullibility as opposed to the greed and guile of the king and the duke make Huck determined not to allow the confidence men to defraud the girls of their patrimony. He tries his best to save the money for them. He has to be extremely cautious because he is dealing with "regular dead beats" and the girls are very naïve. So he explains to Mary Jane his plan to save their property and to punish the impostors. The innocence of the Wilks girls makes Huck follow a very dangerous –

dangerous to himself and to Jim – course of action. Huck is disturbed to see the "miserable girls and niggers hanging around each other's necks and crying," when their fraudulent uncles sell the niggers, separating the children and the mother. He wants to expose the king and the duke right then, but he feels it is not necessary as the sale is illegal and the negroes would return in a week or two.

Huck's last stop is the Phelps plantation. Here he allows Sally Phelps to believe that he is Tom whom she was expecting. Huck and Tom play a number of practical jokes on her and confuse her. Aunt Sally is very affectionate to Huck and forgives him all his pranks. She is worried about his health and when the butter on his head starts melting she suspects he has brain fever. She locks up Huck and Tom to protect them when there was fear of a gang of slave thieves attempting to steal Jim. When Huck is brought home by Silas Phelps after the misadventure of freeing Jim, "Aunt Sally was that glad to see me she laughed and cried both, and hugged me" (215). She "mothered me so good I felt mean, and like I couldn't look her in the face" (218). Aunt Sally keeps vigil all night long for Sid (Tom) when he is involved in freeing Jim. At the end of his long voyage down the river, Huck faces the same situation as at its beginning. He runs away from St. Petersburg to escape the "sivilizing" attempts of Widow Douglas. Now he is afraid that Aunt Sally would adopt him and "sivilize" him. The venue may have changed; the people may be different; but their attitudes are not different. If Huck once again decides "to light out for the Territory" it is because of Aunt Sally.

The ten women whom Huck meets during his voyage have many things in common. They are all Southern white women; they are devout Christians; they believe in the efficacy of prayer; they attend church and perform the Christian rituals. Almost all of them own slaves. Thus they represent the prevailing Southern culture.

In terms of marital status also, they represent all the possibilities: there is a widow, a spinster, three middle-aged married women and five young girls. It may be mentioned in parenthesis that although Emmeline Grangerford died at the age of fifteen, she has a presence in the family through her paintings, elegies, scrap-book etc. Huck admires her sentimental activities.

The middle-aged women, married or not, are anxious to play a mother's role for Huck. All of them wish to take Huck under their protective wings, express concern for his welfare, and try to bring him up according to their lights. Mrs. Loftus expresses a motherly concern for Huck and puts him up a snack to eat on his way to Goshen. She offers to provide escort for his journey as it isn't safe for girls to travel alone at night. From Huck's point of view, the Widow Douglas, Miss Watson and Aunt Sally are in their several ways his tormentors who try to impose their notions of morality and discipline over him. Huck's initial feelings of guilt in aiding Jim to escape are because of the teachings of Miss Watson and her sister and their personal conduct. The second occasion when Huck's conscience pricks him is when the Wilks girls cry over the sale and separation of the negro families. But he knows that the sale would not be legal and that the negroes would rejoin the girls soon. So he is not very much troubled. He is also deeply worried over the defrauding of the girls by the king and the duke and he attempts to pass on the money to the girls even if it meant incurring the wrath of his travelling companions.

Huck might have been a motherless boy. But he lives in a world dominated by mothers in the guise of widows, spinsters, aunts and surrogate mothers. Their concern for Huck is genuine; they want to shape his future in accordance with their values. But Huck has different notions and feels free only outdoors.

Thus, although the women characters have an apparently minimal, or peripheral, role in the scheme of the novel, they influence, unknown to themselves, Huck's thinking, attitudes and actions.

WORKS CITED

Clemens, Samuel Langhorne. *Adventures of Huckleberry Finn*. Norton Critical Editions. New York: W.W. Norton, 1961.

Covici, Pascal, Jr. "Mark Twain and the Feminine." *The New England Quarterly* 66 (1993): 459-464.

Parkison, Jami. "A Woman's Mark Twain." *Mark Twain Journal.* 21:4 (1983): 32-33.

Skandera-Trombley, Laura E. *Mark Twain in the Company of Women.* Philadelphia: University of Pennsylvania Press, 1994.

Stahl, John Daniel. "Mark Twain and Female Power: Public and Private." *Studies in American Fiction* 16:1 (1988): 51-63.

Stein, Regina and Lidston, Robert. "The Mother Figure in Twain's Mississippi Novels." *Mark Twain Journal* 21:4 (1983): 57-58.

Stoneley, Peter. *Mark Twain and the Feminine Aesthetic.* Cambridge: Cambridge University Press, 1992.

Thoreson, Trygve. "'Virtuous According to their Lights': Women in Mark Twain's Early Work." *Mark Twain Journal* 21:4 (1983): 52-56.

Willis, Resa. *Mark and Livy: The Love Story of Mark Twain and the Woman Who Almost Tamed Him.* New York: Atheneum, 1992.

14

'A Supersaturated Solution': Margaret Atwood's Views on Language

Margaret Atwood published a dozen volumes of poetry and another dozen volumes of fiction; she has also written two volumes of non-fiction and scores of book-reviews; she has taught or lectured at many universities. She has been interviewed a number of times on her concerns as a creative writer. She knows two languages, English and French, and she is acquainted with a few more. All this underscores her deep and close involvement with language for nearly sixty years. Not only does she use language for her creative, critical and other work, but she reflects a good deal on the potential and limitations of language. She has articulated her views on language in some of her poems. The problem of communicating through language figures rather prominently in her fiction such as "Giving Birth," *Murder in the Dark*, *The Edible Woman* and *Surfacing*. In fact, some of these are described as "writing about writing." Her verbal medium is the principal focus of some of the interviews she has given. This paper makes an attempt to consider her views on her medium as she expresses them in her poems and interviews. Her comments on this topic in her fiction are not examined here for reasons of space and time.

After this exordium, let us consider Atwood's views on language. First of all, she seems to feel that language is an inescapable legacy for better or worse. For a creative writer, this legacy has severe drawbacks. Atwood writes in "Two-Headed Poems":

> Your language hangs around your neck,
> a noose, a heavy necklace;
> each word is empire
> each word is vampire and mother.
>
> (*Selected Poems II*, 29)

She likens language to a 'noose' around one's neck or a 'heavy necklace'; it is either a threat to one's life which might be lost when the noose is tightened; or it might be a heavy burden though it is an ornament. Each word is as vast as an empire; that is, its connotations could be many like the colonies which make up an empire. In the next line, the poet tells us that 'each word is vampire'. The word, 'vampire' is used not merely for the sake of rhyme, but its use has a significant reason. Vampire is a ruthless, ill-disposed person who preys on others to the extent of sucking their blood when they are asleep. Atwood seems to suggest that words suck the creative writer's blood, figuratively speaking. In the next analogy, each word is 'mother'. While all the preceding four items of comparison, 'noose', 'necklace', 'empire' and 'vampire' imply unpleasant, if not evil, connotations, 'mother' suggests neither unpleasantness nor evil. Like a mother, a word is a source (or origin) of something. This sounds somewhat biblical: "In the beginning was the Word, and the Word was with God, and the Word was God" (St. John 1:1). Thus, it appears that each word is double-edged, evil and beneficent.

The second feature of language which bothers Atwood, as it does many other creative writers, is its inadequacy. She feels that the available word-stock in English is woefully insufficient for her creative purposes. She told an interviewer, Geoff Hancock, in 1986: "Not only is language slippery, but it's limited. The vocabulary we have is limited. There are a lot of things we don't have words for" (Ingersoll 210). In her "Two-Headed Poems," she complains:

> These words slow us, stumble
> in us, numb us, who
> can say even open
> the door, without these diffident
> smiles, apologies?
>
> (*Selected Poems II*, 34)

Atwood appears to notice three unwelcome qualities in available words; (i) they impede a writer's urge to communicate, (ii) they confuse a writer, and (iii) they deaden the sensibility. Hence most writers distrust language. But it is "one of the few tools" of the writers. Atwood concedes: "So we have to use it. We even have to trust it, though it's untrustworthy" (Ingersoll 209).

Margaret Atwood raises a basic question: Is language necessary at all to apprehend reality? How do small babies know the world before they learn a language. She argues, "Cats know the world without language, without what we would call language." So she concludes that language is "one of the most peculiar items that exists" (Ingersoll 209). It is used as an unavoidable tool for communication, yet the writers are aware that it distorts their meaning.

Atwood's dissatisfaction with language is accentuated by her discovery that American Indian languages function differently from English and other European languages. For instance, she found out that one Indian language has no nouns. She told Jim Davidson, an interviewer, in 1978:

> What we would call a noun is a variation of a verb. . .the whole language is composed of verbs. The mode of linguistic expression militates against seeing objects as distinct from their backgrounds. You see the whole field as doing a certain thing: the whole area of your perception

> is behaving in a certain way. There is not a flower sitting on a table; the table is flowering, as it were. It is behaving like a flower in that area of space" (Ingersoll 92).

Atwood complains about the tyrannical stranglehold of nouns in her "Two-Headed Poems":

> We are forced with nouns, nouns
> till our tongues are sullen and rubbery.
> We see this language always
> and merely as a disease
> of the mouth. Also
> as the hospital that will cure us,
> distasteful but necessary.
> (34)

A few lines below, she says:

> Our dreams though
> are of freedom, a hunger
> for verbs (35)

She has said repeatedly that nouns suffocate a writer who seeks a breath of fresh air in verbs.

Atwood attributes the importance of nouns in English to the Lockean tradition which is based on empiricism: "It begins with the noun. It begins with the concrete noun and the concrete verb" (Ingersoll 186). By contrast, the French language, so Atwood thinks, allows more abstract elements. She says: "You can say things in French that sound wimpy in

English" (Ingersoll 186). The fact of the matter is that every writer's freedom of expression is circumscribed by the finite grammatical and lexical resources of the language in which he/she writes. No wonder if Margaret Atwood feels that language is a "noose" or a "vampire."

Yet another point she makes is that words are worn out, a complaint which Ernest Hemingway also voices rather frequently. When the same words are used by many people over and over again, they tend to lose their freshness and flavour. To that extent, they don't convey meaning in a pointed way. Atwood says:

> Language, like the mouths
> that hold and release
> it, it is wet & living, each
>
> word is wrinkled
> with age, swollen
> with other words, with blood, smoothed by
>   numberless
> fresh tongues that have passed across it.
>
> (*Selected Poems II*, 29)

In "Solstice Poem," she is forthright in pointing out the banal effects of such language:

> Worn language clots our throats,
> making it difficult to say
> what we mean, making it
> difficult to see.
>
> (*Selected Poems II*, 44)

Incidentally, Atwood has a dig at political leaders who, in Canada at any rate, speak literally in two tongues, English and French. This is bilingualism in practice. Atwood writes:

> Our leader is a spider
>
> he traps words.
> They shrivel in his mouth,
> he leaves the skins.
> Most leaders speak
> for themselves, then
> for the people.
>
> Who does our leader speak for?
> How can you use two languages
> and mean what you say in both?
>
> (*Selected Poems II*, 30)

There is a link, although Atwood does not provide it, between the triteness of much of the vocabulary and the politician's language. The repetitive use of the same words by politicians of different persuasions which are broadcast by the mass media, again repeatedly, robs such words of their original meaning. In those circumstances, language fails to communicate, or communicate effectively.

A creative writer has to accept language with all its deficiencies and distortions, and work in that medium to achieve his/her aims. The important question now is the interplay between poetry and language. What does poetry do to language? And what does language do to poetry? The first question may seem meaningless to some of us, but there is a two-way influence between poetry and language. An accomplished poet like Atwood addresses this question and comes up with some remarkable observations.

Poetry, explains Atwood, is "a verbal attempt to accomplish something desirable. You can take every poem and trace it back to a source in either prayer, curse, charm or incantation – an attempt to make something happen" (Ingersoll 22).

Autistic children mistake the word for the thing. For instance, if they see the word, "clock," on a piece of paper, they pick it up to see if it ticks. This tendency to mistake words for things, according to Atwood, is "inherent in language in some funny way and poetry is connected with that at some level" (23).

The second point that she makes is that poetry is an aural activity, rather than a 'rational' one. Sound effects are more important to her than the meanings of words: "For me, every poem has a texture of sound which is at least as important to me as the 'argument'. This is not to minimise 'statement'" (Ingersoll 69).

She makes a distinction between writing prose and writing poetry, though both are verbal activities. She says: "I'm a magpie with prose. I collect little pieces of information, overheard conversations. A poem, however, is generated by a word or a phrase."

Her favourite metaphor to describe the interplay between language and poetry is that the former is "a supersaturated solution." Writing poetry is like dipping a thread into it, so crystals form on the thread. "From the language the poem condenses"(105).

Poets are interested in "expansion and elaboration of language." Coining new words, placing words in different contexts and making unusual collocations are some of the linguistic innovations in which the poet is involved and immersed. In this way, old words are invested with new meanings. Atwood observes: "Language changes within our lifetime. As a writer you're part of that process – using an old language, but making new patterns with it. Your choices are numerous" (Ingersoll 112).

If language is essential for poetry, poetry too, in Atwood's view, is essential for language. Poetry renews or rejuvenates language:

> If poetry vanished, language would become dead. It would become embalmed...it's [poetry] the heart of language. If you think of language as a series of concentric circles, poetry is right in the centre. It's where precision takes place. It's where the use of language takes place that can extend a word yet have it be precise (Ingersoll 127).

So, poetry and language are interdependent and mutually supportive. To use Margaret Atwood's own famous expression, the 'survival' of poetry ensures the survival of language. It may be appropriate to conclude by quoting from Margaret Atwood's poem, "Four Small Elegies":

> A language is not words only,
> it is the stories
> that are told in it,
> the stories that are never told.

WORKS CITED

Atwood, Margaret. 1987. *Selected Poems II: Poems Selected & New, 1976-1986*. Boston: Houghton Mifflin Co.

Ingersoll, Earl G. (ed.) 1990. *Margaret Atwood: Conversations*. Princeton, N.J.: Ontario Review Press.

15

Canadian Contribution to Literary Criticism

Canadian literature is about hundred thirty years old; literary criticism is also the same age. In the beginning Canadian critics wrote mainly on British, and occasionally on American, authors. Their orientation was largely British; their method was historical and comparative. Stephen Leacock wrote books on Charles Dickens, O. Henry and Mark Twain; E.K. Broadus wrote *The Poets Laureate in England.* A few Canadian critics wrote on French or German literature also. For instance, A.F.B. Clarke's monumental work, *Boileau and the French Classical Critics in England,* is considered "Canada's most important contribution to the international field" (Pelham, 427). H. Walters wrote a critical work on Heinrich Heine. The critical focus on Canadian literature in the beginning was limited as this literature itself was nascent. E.J. Pratt who was a poet wrote an article on Canadian poetry; Jane M. Turnbull's *Essential Traits of French Canadian Poetry* is a scholarly treatise. Desmond Pacey's *Creative Writing in Canada* and *Ten Canadian Poets,* and Eli Mandel's *Criticism: The Silent Speaking Words* have helped popularise Canadian literature in the last three decades.

Canadian criticism of Canadian literature was initially in the nature of book reviews, histories and surveys. This is understandable because Canadian literature was not only quantitatively small, but it was not considered respectable compared to older European literatures. The non-academic critic, Lorne Pierce, could inspire a group of critics in the twenties with his romantic idealism and nationalism. John Sutherland resisted British influence on Canadian literature; he suspected the cultivated, the cosmopolitan and the urbane as he was rather blunt himself (Ross, 163). The academic critics such as E.K. Brown, A.J.M. Smith and W.E. Collins were polite, but they hardly made clear evaluations. They dared not attack living writers; they praised contemporary poets and undervalued dead writers like Carmen, Lampman and Scott. They had a habit of classification, labelling and pigeon-holing. The positive qualities of their criticism were the comparative and historical method, objectivity and clear exposition of ideas (Pacey 1950, 114).

Northrop Frye is an outstanding Canadian critic with an international reputation. He is influenced by the anthropologist, J.G. Frazer, the psychologist, Carl Jung, and the King James Bible. His major critical works are: *Fearful Symmetry: A Study of William Blake* (1947), *Anatomy of Criticism* (1963) and *The Great Code: The Bible and Literature* (1982). In the second of these, *Anatomy of Criticism*, Frye redefined literature and criticism. This is described as "a marvellous, maddening book".

Frye's critical position is that the principles of literary structure are within literature itself. Criticism can only identify archetypes; literature owes more to other works of literature than to the life and times of the author. One of the cardinal principles of Frye is that myth is "the structural organising principle of literary form". In his view, myth explains the appearance of basic plots and characters in cultures widely separated in time. He likens a critic to a cultural anthropologist, an expert at detecting the presence of mythic patterns in their variously displaced and fragmented forms. A critic's job is to describe and classify and not to evaluate. For Frye, the great encompassing myth of mankind is a circle. At the top of the circle is noon or summer identified with youth and romance. Down below is evening and autumn identified with old age and tragedy. At the bottom of the circle is night or winter identified with death and irony or satire. There is again a new dawn and rebirth identified with spring and comedy (Borklund 216). The advantages of Frye's critical system are its vast sweep which appealed to many critics because it is secular and value-free; it is open at certain critical points (218). Unlike I.A. Richards or Kenneth Burke, Frye does not commit himself to any school of psychology.

Frye's constant dependence on simile and analogy is considered a weak point because analogies do not always have logical validity. If myth is such an important structural principle, why is it that the same myth used by different writers or in different works may or may not move us? (218). Also, Frye tends to use 'genre', 'mode' and 'device' almost synonymously. According to Frye, criticism bears the same relationship to art as history does to action, or philosophy to wisdom. Criticism points out what a given work has in common with others; it does not reveal the qualities which differentiate the work. Thus it places a given work in a context, by defining its mode, its kind and degree of symbolization, the kind of archetypal themes and images it employs, the way it handles words with respect to a real or implied audience or to the writer's relationship to his material. This inevitably makes it like other works. In the demonstration of this likeness lies the critical act.

Northrop Frye's influence may be observed in D.G. James's *Butterfly on Rock* (1970), Margaret Atwood's *Survival* (1972), W.H. New's *Articulating West* (1972), Laurence Ricou's *Virtual Men/ Horizontal World* (1973) and John Mose's *Patterns of Isolation* (1974).

The second outstanding Canadian critic is Marshall McLuhan. Like Frye, he too was a professor of English at the University of Toronto. He was considered the most important thinker since Newton, Darwin, Freud, Einstein and Pavlov (Fekete 135). His detractors brand his ideas McLuhanacy and call his followers McLuhanatics. Praise or detraction, McLuhan made major contributions to literary studies, cultural theory, and to the understanding of the role of the media and technology in society. He was one of the first to recognise that technology had become one of the major factors in human evolution and the changed shape of modern culture (Theall 494). He understood better than many others the interaction of media, culture and technology in the modern world. His fame rests on three important books: *The Mechanical Bride: Folklore of Industrial Man* (1951), *The Gutenberg Galaxy: The Making of Typographic Man* (1962), and *Understanding Media: The Extensions of Man* (1964). In the first of these, McLuhan interprets the products of popular culture and the media industries in a critical or satiric manner. In *The Gutenberg Galaxy*, he analyses the pre-print oral/aural culture and the results of Gutenberg's invention of the movable type and the mass production of books. In this book he predicts the electronic interdependence of the modern world which will blur distinctions between nations. The world will become a "global village" because of the levelling impact of the media. *Understanding Media* examines the radical changes in man's responses caused by electronic communication. He argues that it is the medium which shapes and controls the scale and form of human association and action. Hence he coined the epigram: "the Medium is the Message". There is a four-way pun on the word 'message': 'message', 'massage', 'mess age' and 'mass age'(Fekete 148). *The Gutenberg Galaxy* and *Understanding Media* bridge the historical and theoretical problems of communication, culture and technology. McLuhan, like Frye, is interested in questions of interpretation and symbolism. However, his scope is broader than Frye's as he takes all cultural criticism as his province. He emphasizes the way polysemy in language reveals the continuum of all orders of cultural expression (Theall 494).

McLuhan's insights on Pope, Poe, Pound, Lewis and Joyce are noteworthy. His perceptions are unique. He views the artist as a magician because modern art seeks to control the mind just as primitive art sought to control the external world. He thinks that mass media formed a magical culture. He describes new media as new languages with new and unique powers of expression. McLuhan's contributions to the interface between rapidly developing technology and human culture are significant.

Francis Sparshott, the third important critic, was a professor of philosophy, not of literature like Frye and McLuhan. He explores the common ground between poetry and philosophy; he perceives hidden relations between ideas. He wrote three important books: *The Structure of Aesthetics* (1963), *The Concept of Criticism* (1970) and *The Theory of the Arts* (1982). In the first, he examines the purpose of art criticism and the role of art as an expression of the human condition. In the second book, he argues in favour of the interrelatedness of theories and functions; he also urges the use of reasonable techniques, not 'the one method of criticism.' In the last book which is his *magnum opus* he discusses the aesthetic meta-theory, a theory about the theories of art. Sparshott distinguishes between the classical definition of 'fine arts' and the modern concept of art considered as pure creativity and expressed intuitions. The classical definition regards art as 'a performance with respect to design', as a productivity. He does not believe that the critic's work is somehow more vital than the work he is writing about. He defines criticism as performance, a discourse about performance; it is an art. He argues that a new work of art does not alter the existing order of art, a notion held by T.S. Eliot and Marshall McLuhan. Criticism for him is evaluation based on reasoned discourse (Mandel, 21). Here he differs from Frye who excludes evaluation from the province of criticism. Evaluation implies standards of value which depend on theories of value which, in turn, depend on the social or metaphysical content. In Sparshott's view "critical acitvity seeks and finds, if it does not create, experience that is worth dwelling on. The old fear that criticism might dissolve enjoyment has no ground.

Only mindless enjoyment could thus be melted, and mindless enjoyment is never enough for people with minds" (177).

Margaret Atwood, the next major critic in Canada, is both a creative writer and a critic. She was a student of Northrop Frye. She is brilliant, witty, persuasive and insightful. Her *Survival: A Thematic Guide to Canadian Literature* (1972) is an influential study of the collective literary imagination and of the key patterns that constitute the shape of Canadian literature which can afford clues to the national consciousness. She argues that every culture has a central symbol that functions like a code of beliefs, an idea derived from Frye's theories. In her view, the central image of Canadian culture is that of a collective victim struggling for survival, an image of both a hostile natural environment and a colonial history. A consequence of this is that the national psychology is fatalistic, the expression of a victim mentality. Mere survival becomes a central concern in the midst of crisis and disasters such as blizzards and wrecks, of onslaughts of other cultures. The French Canadians feel threatened by the Anglo-Saxon culture; the English Canadians feel insecure because of the powerful impact of American culture. The land was hard and the country was an exploited colony. Atwood identifies some archetypal images in Canadian literature: nature as a monster, animals as victims, Indians as the persecuted, the Artist as the Paralyzed, and Woman as Ice Maiden or Absent

Venus. The Wordsworthian or Thoreauvian notions of Nature as a beneficent power are not valid in Canada in Atwood's view. The landscape and the climate are both forbidding. Water and snow which are plentiful are often killers as drowning and freezing are common. Canada was founded on the fur trade which implies skinning the animal which feels threatened. In a similar way, Canadians feel threatened by others, notably the Americans, who go to Canada to hunt in a metaphoric, if not in a literal, way. The Canadians' identification with the animals in the battle for survival is the expression of a deep-seated cultural fear. As Atwood puts it "For the Canadian animal bare survival is the main aim in life, failure as an individual is inevitable, and extinction as a species is a distinct possibility." The first inhabitants of Canada, the Indians and the Eskimos, are either victims of the White immigrants, or tormentors of their own tribes. The settlers imposed an order on a labyrinthine, complex, curved Nature through symmetrical geometric shapes. In a sense, the Canadian pioneer is a square peg in a round hole. Even the family does not provide comfort and security to a Canadian; it traps him. The Canadian writer may stay in the culture and be crippled as an artist; he may escape into nothing; or he may write from the centre of the dilemma. Another interesting feature of Canadian literature, as Atwood finds it, is that old women past fifty are heroines in Canadian literature. They are tough, sterile, granite-jawed women. They are often malevolent, sinister or life-denying. There is no Venus figure or goddess of love, sex and fertility in Canadian literature. The sense of doom inherent in Calvinism and the feeling of powerlessness implied in Colonialism have always fed one another making death the central Canadian experience.

For a literature which is hundred thirty years old, the critical achievement of Canada is very impressive. It is original, insightful and stimulating. It has achieved world reputation in the work of Frye and McLuhan.

WORKS CITED

Borklund, Elmer. "Northrop Frye" in *Contemporary Literary Critics*. London: St. James Press, 1977. 212-218.

Edgar, Pelham. "Literary Criticism in Canada". *University of Toronto Quarterly*. (1939).

Fekete, John. *The Critical Twilight*. London: Routledge and Kegan Paul, 1977.

Mandel, Eli. (ed.) *Contexts of Canadian Criticism*. Chicago and London: University of Chicago Press, 1971. "Introduction". 3-25.

McNamara, Eugene. (ed.) *The Interior Landscape: The Literary Criticism of Marshall McLuhan*. New York: McGraw-Hill. 1971 [1969].

Pacey, Desmond. "Literary Criticism in Canada". *University of Toronto Quarterly* (1950). 113-119.

__________ . "The Course of Canadian Criticism" in *Literary History of Canada*, III. 2 edn. (Gen Ed.). Carol F. Klinck. Toronto and Buffalo: University of Toronto Press, 1965. 16-31.

Ross, Malcolm. "Critical Theory: Some Trends" in *Literary History of Canada*, III. 2 edn. (Gen Ed.). Carol F. Klinck.

Sparshott, Francis. "Art and Criticism" in *Contexts of Canadian Criticism*. (ed.) Eli Mandel. 1971. pp. 154-177.

Sullivan, Rosemary. "Survival" in *Literary History of Canada*, III. 2 edn. (Gen Ed.). Carol F. Klinck.

Theall, Donald. "Marshall McLuhan" in *Literary History of Canada*, III. 2 edn. (Gen Ed.). Carol F. Klinck.

Trott, Elizabeth. "Francis Edward Sparshott" in *Literary History of Canada*, III. 2 edn. (Gen Ed.). Carol F. Klinck.